William Charles Edmund Newbolt

Penitence and peace

being addresses on the fifty-first and twenty-third psalms

William Charles Edmund Newbolt

Penitence and peace
being addresses on the fifty-first and twenty-third psalms

ISBN/EAN: 9783337003197

Printed in Europe, USA, Canada, Australia, Japan

Cover: Foto ©Lupo / pixelio.de

More available books at **www.hansebooks.com**

BY THE SAME AUTHOR.

Crown 8vo. 2s. 6d.

THE FRUIT OF THE SPIRIT. Being Ten Addresses bearing on the Spiritual Life.

Small 8vo. 1s. 6d.

THE MAN OF GOD. Being Six Addresses delivered during Lent at the Primary Ordination of the Right Rev. the Lord Alwyne Compton, Bishop of Ely.

Crown 8vo. 2s. 6d.

THE VOICE OF THE PRAYER-BOOK. Being Spiritual Addresses bearing on the Book of Common Prayer.

LONDON & NEW YORK:
LONGMANS, GREEN, & CO.

PENITENCE AND PEACE

BEING ADDRESSES

on the

FIFTY-FIRST AND TWENTY-THIRD PSALMS

BY THE REV.

W. C. E. NEWBOLT, M.A.

Canon and Chancellor of St. Paul's
Examining Chaplain to the Lord Bishop of Ely

LONDON

LONGMANS, GREEN, & CO.

AND NEW YORK: 15 EAST 16th STREET

1892

TO

MY OLD STUDENTS

AT THE THEOLOGICAL COLLEGE, ELY,

WHO TAUGHT ME

MORE THAN I TAUGHT THEM,

THIS BOOK

IS

AFFECTIONATELY DEDICATED.

Preface

THESE addresses are published in answer to requests which have been made from time to time by those who heard them delivered. They were first spoken to those preparing for Holy Orders in the Theological College at Ely. And I have thought it best to retain the special character and allusions which necessarily belong to addresses of that kind, rather than rearrange them as for a wider audience.

The nature of the appeal made in them, and the circumstance of their original delivery, must be my excuse for their purely hortatory language, and for a certain abruptness of style.

I assume that both the fifty-first and twenty-third psalms were written by David.

My reason for using the Prayer-book Version of the fifty-first psalm is chiefly that this version has become so very familiar to us from its liturgical use. The Bible Version of the twenty-third psalm, on the other hand, has been adopted, not without misgivings, chiefly for some turns of expression in it, which lent themselves to the object of the addresses.

W. C. E. N.

3, AMEN COURT, E.C.,
April 28, 1892.

Contents

PSALM LI.

		PAGE
I.	The Exceeding Sinfulness of Sin	1
II.	The Complete Acceptance of the Penitent	15
III.	The Reparation of Sin's Ravages	28
IV.	The Life of Restored Usefulness	39
V.	Sion and Jerusalem	52
VI.	The Sacrifice of Righteousness	64

PSALM XXIII.

I.	The Good Shepherd the Protector of Life	77
II.	The Good Shepherd the Refuge from the World	90
III.	The Good Shepherd the Defender from Sin	102
IV.	The Good Shepherd the Stay of the Soul in Death	115
V.	The Good Shepherd our Help in Trouble	131
VI.	The Good Shepherd our Companion for Ever	142

Grant, we beseech Thee, merciful Lord, to Thy faithful people pardon and peace, that they may be cleansed from all their sins, and serve Thee with a quiet mind; through Jesus Christ our Lord. Amen.

PENITENCE
Psalm LI.

"Bonum mihi, quia humiliasti me, ut discam justificationes Tuas."

I.

"Have mercy upon me, O God, after Thy great goodness: according to the multitude of Thy mercies do away mine offences. Wash me throughly from my wickedness: and cleanse me from my sin. For I acknowledge my faults: and my sin is ever before me. Against Thee only have I sinned, and done this evil in Thy sight: that Thou mightest be justified in Thy saying, and clear when Thou art judged. Behold, I was shapen in wickedness, and in sin hath my mother conceived me. But lo, Thou requirest truth in the inward parts: and shalt make me to understand wisdom secretly."—Ps. li. 1-6.

THIS is the psalm which, of all inspired compositions (with the one exception of the Lord's Prayer), has been repeated most often by the Church. For many hundreds of years it was said daily, except at certain special times, in each of the seven offices. And if we examine it, we shall see that we owe to it many theological and liturgical phrases, such as "Lord, have mercy," "the clean heart," "the broken and contrite heart;" or, once more, " O

Lord, open Thou our lips; and our mouth shall shew forth Thy praise." While here, above all, is a clear revelation of that Holy Spirit, Whose sanctifying, indwelling grace is such a force in the New Testament revelation.[1] But quite apart from this, who could enumerate the thousands and thousands of penitents whose sorrow has found vent in these blessed words? Well might the great commentator say, "O most happy fault, which has brought in so many straying sheep to the good Shepherd!"

For this psalm has been associated with David's penitence, after his act of deceit, murder, and adultery in the case of Bathsheba, the wife of Uriah the Hittite. And the psalm has been divided into five portions.[2] The first (verses 1-6) representing the humble self-abasement of the sinner; the second (verses 7, 8) setting forth the grounds of confidence in the mercies of God; the third (verses 9-12) containing the prayer that God would turn away His face from David's sin; the fourth (verses 13-17) setting forth the encouragement that would be vouchsafed to sinners by his pardon; while the last divi-

---

[1] See Dr. Neale, Commentary on this Psalm.
[2] See Dr. Neale, *in loc.*

sion (verses 18–19) seems to portray the rise of the Catholic Church, which even then he had begun to look for.

These, at all events, may form a sort of framework from which to examine this psalm, so deeply spiritual, so full of meaning, so adapted to the needs of all penitent sinners.

And, when we are thinking over a psalm like this, do not let us think that it is going too low, for us who are come here out of the world, to draw very near to God. If we trace up the sins which we have recorded on our last self-examination list, we shall be startled to find how they are in so many cases trailing fibrous offshoots from the tree of the deadly sins, only just kept in check. That impatient word draws its malignity from the stock of anger; that evil imagination has thrust in its tearing thorns like some pushing briar, cropping up from the tree of impurity. Indolence goes back to sloth, self-indulgence to gluttony. We need not fear to go too low; the Church evidently did not fear to do so, when she prescribed the frequent use of words like these, charged as they undoubtedly are with the deepest penitence.

I.

First of all, then, we seem to trace in these verses this thought—the nature of sin in the eyes of one who sees God. It had all been carried out so successfully. It was a complete sin; there was the temptation, the delight in the temptation, the consent of the will, and then the act. The result of it is all summed up in that mournful verse, "And when the mourning was past, David sent and fetched her to his house, and she became his wife, and bare him a son. But the thing that David had done displeased the Lord."[1] It was all done. God had seen it, noted it down; and now what was the result? Hear how the words pour out fast and thick: "offence," "wickedness," "sin," "fault," an abiding presence of sin, as "evil;" an outraged God, an inward corruption.

How terrible it is that we should have it in our power to put the whole course of life out of gear! Just as one crime against the State can set all the machinery of our civilization against us, on which our existence now runs so smoothly; and the network of law,

---

[1] 2 Sam. xi. 27.

which secured us freedom of motion in the right path, serves only to trip us up when we have left it; so, one great act of sin against God has the power to pervert all the spiritual relationships of our life. David is feeling here the awful truth, that there is no more fearful punishment for sin than sin itself; in its heavy burden, it is an anticipation of the sharpest pang of hell, the *pœna damni*, the cutting off from the presence of God. God is offended; a blow is struck against His Majesty; the path of His approach is blocked. Prayer is impossible; Holy Communion would be a profanation; meditation a mockery. Adam hides himself from the presence of God.

It is wickedness; the whole thing has been the spell of some hideous fascination, like witchcraft. It is sin, an injury maiming my whole life. It is a fault, a crack, a jar; just that tiny hole drilled in the bell, which for ever takes from it the clearness of its tone. My character, or at least my self-respect, is broken; penitence is very beautiful, but it is not innocence. And this must be ever before me, in so many ways; the weakness in the presence of temptation betrays the once broken will. The sinful memory, ringing with peals of ribald and mocking laughter, haunts my still hours. The abiding punishment of God marks the crooked limb still unstraitened; the loss of self-respect, and even of the respect of others, is a mournful testimony to a moral collapse. Sin goes through the world armed with its own punishment: and all its malice is enumerated here; from the offence which is directed against God, to the fault which injures the integrity of my life.

In an ethical study by a popular writer, in the form of a story; at a critical moment the heroine is vouchsafed a vision of a successful sin in all its hideous nature, and shrinks back appalled. David sees it here, but, alas! too late to save his life from the shadow which never again left it.

II.

But it would seem as if sin were thus exhibited in all its bearings, and painted in its darkest colours, as if to show us that where iniquity did abound, grace did much more abound. The penitent, having laid bare his sin, now asks for God's grace. And first of all he asks for mercy. What a depth of meaning there is, at all events to English-speaking people, in the word which we thus put into the psalm! When the foe lay vanquished in the power of the conqueror, to cry, "Mercy!" meant to cry, "Ransom!"— "Spare my life and take a ransom!"[1] What a meaning it may have to us if, when we cry, "Mercy!" we feel that we are asking God to take a ransom!—

> "Beata cujus brachiis
> Pretium pependit saeculi,
> Statera facta est corporis
> Praedam tulitque Tartari."

This must ever be the cry of the penitent sinner. "The soul that sinneth it shall die;" but He in His pity allows me to plead those precious merits, and so obtain pardon and peace.

But he goes on to ask God to do away his offences; to "blot them out," as we read elsewhere. Sin remains as a witness against us, and only God can blot it out. There is a red line which He draws across it —the writing of a Saviour's blood. This is what we mean by Absolution. Perhaps we

[1] See Richardson's English Dictionary, under "Mercy."

hardly think enough about this; we think a great deal of the shame and agony of confession, but do we think enough of all that is meant by Absolution? Do we feel that here is the relief of a great burden; the laying aside of every weight which hinders our onward course? In the well-known creation of the great novelist, the ghost who appears to the earth-bound miser comes in dragging behind him the chain of title-deeds and cash-boxes, as the sign of a long life buried in the world. We, too, carry a chain; we little think that a weakness in character is owing to some weight pressing on it from far back in boyhood. We little think that our inability to mount up comes from a weight which clogs our heels. Why should we go heavily while the enemy oppresseth us? Why should we have to pay the yearly tax of our best hopes and aims to the monster who lies curled up within, called "Habit"? Why should we go in fear and dread before God? David knew better when he said, "Do away mine offences." And this is what God offers to do, did we but believe it.

But David goes even further. It is a bold prayer, an awful prayer: "Wash me throughly "—more and more. "*Amplius lava me.*" Have we courage to pray thus? Did David see the sword which was henceforth never to leave his home? Did he see the grief to be brought upon him by Absalom, by Adonijah, by the son of Zeruiah; and all the misery of rebellion, and the indignity of his banishment? Have we courage to say, "more and more"? Alas! we soon cry out. We find Lent and its discipline hard. What shall we do if God sees fit to make all our life a Lent, in the secrets of His love to us; a Lent of sickness, sorrow, or failure? The terrible prevalence of suicide is more than a passing phenomenon; it means souls snapping here and there under God's correction. "Happy is the man whom God correcteth." Yes, it is hard for the soldier on the battle-field to lose his right arm, but he welcomes the sharp knife if it is to save his life. David was never the same man again. Never mind; the life of pain was better than the dull narcotic of sin. "More and more"—it is a sign of true penitence.

"Minds which verily repent
Are burdened with impunity,
And comforted by chastisement.

> That punishment's the best to bear
> That follows soonest on the sin;
> And guilt's a game where losers fare
> Better than those who seem to win."[1]

If we can welcome punishment, if we can embrace the sword, if we can expiate our sins by a lifelong cross, we ought to be glad. "Wash me more and more, and cleanse me."

III.

It only remains for us to notice the grounds on which he asks for pardon. In the first place, there is the multitude of God's mercies. Each day we live is an argument in our favour. God sent me here; God has rescued me so often; God is always helping me; though I fall, I shall not be cast away. Hope is a great power. We seem like people forced to climb higher and higher up the face of the cliff, by the sea driven in before the gale. It seems impossible to climb any further, and the spray is dashing in their faces, and the rock quivers to its base, as the waves are shivered upon it. And then they find, it may be, at their feet, grass and flowers in the cleft of the rock, which could only grow

---

[1] Quoted from "Eternal Hope," Archdeacon Farrar.

above the highest water-mark, and at once they feel there is hope, and with hope comes an access of strength. So there are flowers in the lives of all of us here, which could only grow at a height above the devouring level of mortal sin. Let us hope.

And further, he has told God everything; he has concealed nothing. "I acknowledge my faults." Further, he acknowledges the true relation of sin to God. It is not the injury done to Uriah or to society; it is the insult done to God. "Against Thee only have I sinned."

And further, God knows how weak we are. "Behold, I was shapen in wickedness;" and therefore "the truth in the inward parts" can only be reached when the plenitude of mercy touches the magnitude of sin.

Indeed, it would be something if we could gauge the depth of sin this Lent. You are going out to grapple with it. It will be yours to see its insidious growth in the child who passes under your hands. It will be yours to be baffled by its malignant intensity, as it seems to leap over, with its devouring flame, sacraments, prayers, and all spiritual barriers, in some cases in which you are interested. As you pass through the world, you will be like one travelling up the sides of a volcano: if you thrust your stick beneath the surface of society, you will find a scorching furnace underneath.

Men and women will come to you, in agony and despair. What if you know nothing of the diagnosis of sin! It is so wonderful that God has put His absolving power into the hands of men, that they may give sympathy as well as guidance.

Truly there is enough to make us solemn, earnest, self-denying, this Lent.

I want to see the mystery of sin.

I want to know something about sin in myself.

II.

"Thou shalt purge me with hyssop, and I shall be clean: Thou shalt wash me, and I shall be whiter than snow. Thou shalt make me hear of joy and gladness: that the bones which Thou hast broken may rejoice."—Ps. li. 7, 8.

IF in the preceding verses we endeavoured to see something of the exceeding sinfulness of sin, in those two verses we may see rather the fulness of the acceptance of the penitent. If we look into them, we shall see many mysteries opening up before us. And one glance will tell us a significant fact, which lies on the very surface—that the imagery of the acceptance, the details, so to speak, of the pardon, are taken from the ceremonies employed in purifying the sufferer from that most loathsome, most deadly disease, leprosy, whose lingering corruption has been called a very sacrament of sin.

This is a startling truth, as we stand showing to God our broken life; that sin of which we think so lightly—that weakness, as we are pleased to call it; that sin of which we hardly feel ashamed; that sin which we acknowledge as it were with a tender self-disparagement, which suggests a delicate veil of humility, toning down the abrupt colouring of a character otherwise, perhaps, too crude; the confession which "blesses with faint blame." God calls this leprosy.

He is treating us for leprosy. In the sad story of a great invention, when the wife, a stranger to her husband's grand purpose, and ignorant of his life's work, had let in the rough mob to break his model, and wreck the fruit of patient years of hardly won discovery; when she points out to him the shapeless mass lying at his feet, he only said out of his broken heart, "You have done foolishly." What can we think that it costs God, our loveless word, our wayward action, our repeated offence? It means the breaking down of long years of patient construction, of gentle struggling with our infirmities. Well do we call it a fall, a fault, an offence! He too in His tenderness says, "You have done foolishly," and proceeds to work our cure. But it is full of difficulty; its greatness is the measure of our fault. There is this aspect to all the ordinances of the Church. The Altar, with its tender and sublime memories, at the same time represents and continues the sacrifice due to sin. The Font at the very entrance of the church speaks of a death unto sin. Confirmation suggests a need of strength. Penance presupposes falls. The clergy in our midst tell of wounds and bruises and putrefying sores. As "the Son of God goes forth to war," as the Church marches on her way "terrible as an army with banners,"[1] our eyes light on the physicians, and the ambulance-train, and the grim realities of the conflict which they imply to us. If God is to deliver us, and cleanse us from our sins, the greatness of the remedy is in proportion to the soreness of the disease.

I.

The cleansing of the leper which David here refers to is full of significance. The priest had to take two birds,[2] and of them to

---

[1] Cant. vi. 4.
[2] See Bonar, "Leviticus," p. 257, etc.; and Wordsworth on Lev. xiv.

slay one, and let the blood fall into an earthen vessel over running water. Then he had to take cedar-wood, scarlet wool, and hyssop, and bind them on the living bird, and dip them in the blood and water, and with them sprinkle the leper seven times, and then let the living bird loose in the open field.

Can anything be more significant? The two birds to be taken speak of Him Who is of two natures, human and Divine. The cedar-wood speaks of the fragrant wood of the cross. The hyssop, the lowly plant used for purifying, sets forth the personal application of Christ's pardon to the soul. The scarlet is the royal robe of Him Who "reigns from the tree." And these are all bound to the living bird, typical of the Divine nature in Christ, from Whom all ordinances derive their significance. And then there is the sprinkling of the blood and water on the penitent, and the living bird carries away the taint, as it were, with him, in his escape to the open field. Truly as we gaze upon the Cross, shining more and more clearly through the symbols, we see His figure bending towards us; we hear Him saying, "This is He that came by water and blood."[1]

[1] 1 S. John v. 6.

Contrition has brought the penitent to the priest; confession has brought him to the sevenfold sprinkling of blood and water, with scarlet and hyssop dipped in the blood of the dead bird, attached to the living bird; and the leper rises up, cleansed, purified, restored, to take again his privileges to which God has once more admitted him.

And whatever privileges the leper might claim in the letter, we may claim in the spirit; our defilement is one, and our restoration shall be one. Contrition, confession, amendment on the part of the sinner, shall be met on the side of God with Absolution, inward purity, and restoration to favour and strength. Just as the leper was cut off from the dead past, so Absolution breaks the chain which binds us. As the leper in the signs of his purification recognized the sweetness and purity of a restored nature, so in God's forgiveness we recognize the earnest of the restored temple of our life. As the leper could once more move among his fellow-men, so we can move amongst others, without that haunting humiliation, "Ah! if they knew all!" I am not ashamed of what I was, being what I am.

II.

"Thou shalt purge me with hyssop." Do we quite believe it? It may be, on some Church festival we have sat down to watch the great procession of the saints sweeping by us in all its magnificence, or have taken up the record of some simple life, and have seen the common things of an everyday existence lit up with supernatural brilliancy, and idealized with saintliness, and have wistfully asked, "Why cannot I attain unto it?" Why do I cast down in despair image after image of a distorted holiness, veneered with a false sentiment, and daubed with unreal piety? Cleanliness! Is it that? Just the first step? Cleaning, scouring, cleansing! Without a stroke of grander work, with no growing outline or developing image—cleanliness?

"Thou shalt purge me with hyssop, and I shall be *clean*."

Those specks of dust, those smears, those begrimed habits, they make holiness impossible. Clean! But is it not this that I have longed for? Did the guilty queen herself moan with an intenser longing, "What, will these hands ne'er be clean?"

"*With hyssop.*" Do we quite believe it? That the hyssop is bound to the scarlet robe of the King, and tied to the cedar of the cross, and dipped in the blood and water, and bound up with the living bird, —the Divine nature of Jesus Christ? Do we quite believe it, that we can have something more to help us, beyond the strong resolution, so often broken; more than the effort of our own will — the grace of the blood of Jesus Christ Himself, to help us to overcome the old sin, the old weakness, to remove the old shame, which we hide from God; like the Spartan boy, who would let the stolen animal, which he clasped within the folds of his dress, tear out his vitals, rather than extract a confession of unsuccessful guilt?

There is the hyssop; there are sprays of it in the hand of every priest. Why are we not purified; why are we not free? We are sprinkled with it, indeed, at every service— "that those things may please Him, which we do at this present." We may not presume to pass out of the tainted atmosphere of our daily walk into His presence without it. But penitence is too great, too personal a thing, to take place in the public service. "In the mean time," says the Prayer-book, before presenting ourselves to God at the Altar; the self-examination, the contrition, the confession, the amendment, must all be done; and even then we shall need sprinkling before we enter on the service of the sanctuary. Why, then, are we not free? Why should cleanliness be the one thing needful, and so often the one thing wanting? "And I shall be clean." Who can tell, but he who has had the blood-stained hands and defiled heart, what it is to be clean? Let us think only of the refreshment of it—clean!

"*Unde, quo, quomodo?*" is traced over the door which admits to the priesthood. "Whence comest thou?" says God, when we stand before Him. And the journey, it may be, has been a long one, and the roads by which we have reached our present purpose have been black and dusty. Ah! as I think of it all, it seems more and more hopeless. That first sin, long, long ago. The shame I felt, the fall of it, when I shut my eyes and jumped out into the night, and lay bleeding, crushed, and begrimed. And then, as I crawled up again, how different it all was! Could I say my prayers? Is not prayer a mockery; God heareth not sinners? On the next Sunday, I heard God walking in the cool of the garden, and I was afraid, and hid myself. And my feet were bleeding with bristling thorns; and I pushed my way amidst briars and thistles.

This knowledge of good and evil! Who said Satan was a liar? He promised that I should be a God, that I should know. And what do I know? My own shame. And then came Confirmation—alas! the sin was there all the time; then the first Communion, but still it was there; when good resolutions struck down on to that caked dirt, hard as rock, they died. "By the waters of Babylon we sat down and wept, when we remembered thee, O Sion."

It would be a blessing indeed to be quite clean. And, indeed, to us, who hope to be priests, it is essential. We have to undertake the delicate work of the ministry, to move amidst the tender workmanship and spotless purity of heavenly things, to handle sacraments, to study the minds and writings of the saints, to use their prayers, to deal with saintly souls, to bear to sinners the unsearchable riches of Christ. "*Unde, quo, quomodo?*" A taint from the past, a smear of an old sin, a clod from the defilement of youth, may mar our work. "Be ye clean, that bear the vessels of the Lord."[1]

III.

But he takes us higher. "Whiter than snow." More than cleansed: white—whiter than snow; that is, something to be afraid of defiling, something to fear falling away from; not a mere pall of whiteness, hiding corruption beneath, to be trodden down by the busy traffic of life, but in itself white and pure, attracting the rays of heavenly love. In the days of the martyrdoms, it is said that a Christian the night before his suffering fell asleep in his prison, and dreamed a dream of Paradise. He was walking in a garden of delight, where all was made of the purest transparent glass, clear as crystal. The trees glanced and flashed as they waved their boughs, the ground sparkled and shone; and the people themselves, who moved up and down there, they were of glass too; but as he went along his way, he noticed that

[1] Isa. lii. 11.

hands were pointed at him in amazement. Men shrunk from him in horror, and he looked. He was of glass as well; and on his breast was a dark spot, a shadow amidst all this light. In an agony of shame he clasped his hands over the place. In vain! they also were of glass, and the defilement shone through them. And he remembered that he was not in charity with a fellow-Christian; some trifling difference he had thought it, but it was a dark spot in Paradise, and a strange spectacle among the blessed. He sent for him, he asked his pardon; he was called to Paradise. If a Christian could feel thus of an act or thought simply wanting in charity, what of our whiteness; what of our hearts?

"Oh that our lives, which flee so fast,
   In purity were such,
That not an image of the past
   Should fear that pencil's touch!
Retirement then might hourly look
   Upon a soothing scene;
Age steal to its allotted nook
   Contented and serene,
With hearts as calm as lakes that sleep,
   In frosty moonlight glistening;
Or mountain rivers, where they creep,
Along a channel broad and deep,
   To their own far-off murmurings listening."

"Whiter than snow," in view of the past,—this is indeed a mercy. "Whiter than snow," in view of the future,—this is indeed a promise.

IV.

But he takes us higher still. "That the bones which Thou hast broken may rejoice." We are now in view of a most blessed truth—that the very places where we were weakest, the very places where our bones gave way, may become our strongest points, our joy and gladness. Do not let us cower before our besetting sin. The broken limbs of our life may yet be sources of joy. Selfishness may be so completely crushed out as to leave us the real virtue of self-respect. Cowardice, which shrunk from danger, may lead us, still feeling the danger, to be the first to meet it. Faults of temper, want of self-control, undisciplined life, indolence,—in all these points, where we sink back beaten, we may yet rejoice. Is not this something for us to do this Lent? The hyssop and the washing away of sin; the brilliancy and the whiteness of virtue; the joy and gladness of

Importance of Above Considerations.

a reinvigorated life. It is an awful responsibility to carry God's message. For if we ask, "Who shall ascend into the hill of the Lord: or who shall rise up in His holy place? the answer comes back clear and distinct, "He that hath clean hands, and a pure heart."[1]

[1] Ps. xxiv. 3, 4.

III.

"Turn Thy face from my sins: and put out all my misdeeds. Make me a clean heart, O God: and renew a right spirit within me. Cast me not away from Thy presence: and take not Thy Holy Spirit from me. O give me the comfort of Thy help again: and stablish me with Thy free Spirit."—Ps. li. 9-12.

WE may, perhaps, trace in these verses the expression of a wish on the part of David; in the accents of his heart-broken prayer, that the *effect* of his sin may be done away. He would be a sanguine man who should think this possible in one sense; for some sins pass so quickly out of our control, that we speedily lose all restraint over them. It is a simple thing just to scatter the firebrands, but the fire soon gets beyond our reach. An infidel writer may issue his book, and live and die; but when can his account be said to be finished, as age after age drinks in the poison? Just a turn of the foot loosened the speck of snow; but now it is thundering in an avalanche down the slope; and a village is in ruins.

But David means rather the effect of sin on himself. For it is a sad truth, that the malice of even pardoned sin is not quite done away. Even after the washing there may yet remain a taint; after the hyssop still some lingering predisposition to evil. "Simon, son of Jonas, lovest thou Me?"[1] The limb broken by a threefold denial, still needed strengthening by a painful and humiliating process. The broken piece of porcelain, however skilfully mended, does not ring quite true; it is never of the same value again. The broken limb, however skilfully set, is sometimes troublesome under certain atmospheric conditions. There are twinges, a half giving way, and painful struggle in the presence of old temptation. So David's prayer here is for more than forgiveness, more than remission of punishment, more than abolition of sin; it is for restoration to what he was before.

I.

And see! he can count on the wonderful patience of God. "Turn Thy face from my

[1] S. John xxi. 15.

sins." He does not hesitate to ask God to forget it all; to forget the rude request for the portion of goods, the home left, the squandered property, the being driven in to God, unwilling and degraded.

> "Come to thy God in time,
> Rings out Tintagel's chime;
> Youth, manhood, old age past,
> Come to thy God *at last.*"

And all this to be as if it had never been! Is this possible? In one sense, yes; in another sense, no. Think only how we have altered our lives. It is said to have been the constant prayer of a very holy man, "O my God, make me what I might have been if I never had sinned!" How different our lives are to that which God meant them to be! Before now, we have opened the west door of some splendid Gothic cathedral, and have gazed in, where the vanishing perspective and soaring arches make it like a vision of heaven as it appeared to the prophet: "Thine eyes shall see the King in His beauty: they shall behold the land *of distances.*"[1] And as we look nearer, we see marks of ruin and incompleteness, wonderfully seized upon by

[1] Isa. xxxiii. 17.

the builder's skill, and woven into one artistic whole. Here the Norman solidity melts into the delicate gracefulness of the Early English, which in turn is seized upon and covered with ornament by the Decorated, and varied here and there by a Tudor window, or panelling Perpendicular. Here the great tower came crashing down, and its reconstruction in another style has become the main feature of the building. It is so with our life, looked at by the outside observer; it has a character, it has those who respect it and love it. But we know the secret of its growth—how it is made up of restored failures and reconstructed catastrophes, by the wonderful patience of God, Who has made the very props and stays by which He has buttressed up our tottering life, beautiful.

We can never be the same as if we had never sinned, but He in His great mercy will let us forget the history of the formation of our character. We shall do very well for rough work; perhaps, as far as the world goes, we shall get on better. We shall be more men of the world, as they like to think, less in conspiracy with a too exacting spirituality, which they label dangerous, under the name of "sacerdotalism." The past is an awful subject, the steps by which we have reached what we are. Yes, God will forget it, turn His face from it, blot it out. Ought we? Should we not rather sometimes steal up to that bruised and bleeding Form, and say—

> "Oh! make me feel it was my sin,
> As if no other sin were there,
> That was to Him Who bears the world
> A load that He could scarcely bear"?

Sometimes when we are in despair, and seem to be making so little progress, may we not look back and say, "Well, I am moving; see what I have passed on the banks"? Sometimes when we are tempted to be harsh and censorious, may we not recall ourselves by that which God tells us: "Love ye therefore the stranger: for ye were strangers in the land of Egypt"?[1] Sometimes when our hearts are cold and perfunctory, when the sermons we preach are dry, and the services distasteful, and we contemptuously ask what this handful of rustics can know about the strong interests of the spiritual life, then we should do well to recall what God has been

[1] Deut. x. 19.

to us, and warm up to tell them of pardon, peace, and acceptance. Yes, God will forget all; He is very patient. God will blot out; we shall be a building of some kind, a restoration, only never quite what we might have been. Some of the Jews every Friday go to a place in Jerusalem, known as the Jews' wailing-place, where there are just a few foundation-stones of the old temple, and there lament their fallen greatness. There are wailing-places, it may be, and always will be, in our own lives. But a new city has risen up, and new duties and new hopes, and God has promised to forget.

II.

He goes on further to ask for restoration to strength, as shown in the clean heart and right spirit. The clean heart being a desire for right things in the seat of the affections; the right spirit being a susceptibility to heavenly influence in the seat of the conscience, the inner man.

There is a terrible liking for sin sometimes, a disposition to it, like the craving of the drunkard, a going out to meet temptation.

When Satan came to our blessed Lord, there was no hand stretched out from within to meet the temptation halfway; whereas when Eve was tempted, the eye had already gone out to see the tree that it was to be desired to make one wise, her ear to drink in the flattery. Perhaps we priests need more than we think the clean heart in this sense. We shall have possibly to mix in all manner of difficult surroundings, in our professional capacity. We shall have to meet worldly men, and be very often within reach of pursuits which once were very absorbing, and of intense interest to us, but which now we feel to be unclerical. It is possible that we may have to read as a duty sceptical books, or be placed by God in a position which is a constant temptation to us; or old sins may come back in other ways. The old conceit which haunted us at school may turn us into that contemptible creature known as the popular preacher. The service of God may minister to our pride, as our voice goes ringing down the aisle, or the church seems filled after hard visiting in the parish, or other exertion on our part. Surely it is a time now in which to renew those holy impressions that have faded from us in the rough contact with the world. What higher joy can we have than to be busied about holy things—about God, His Holy Word, His Sacraments, the souls of men, the death-bed? And if we do not care for these things, ought we not to educate our spirit? There was a time when men called the Alps a barbarous and savage scene; and now they climb just for once to catch their inspiration, and gaze on their majesty. It is possible to educate our taste; rather it is a renewal of what once has been. It is possible to get back the awe of our childhood's prayers, and the earnestness of our childhood's grace before meals; it is possible to get back something of the ignorance of sin, which is the dearly coveted gift of innocence. At least we can refuse to keep up the knowledge of it.

What a mistake men make who read all sorts and kinds of literature, as if they had a right to do so! It is a great mistake in any one, but fatal in a priest. We lose thereby that delicacy of touch, so essential to an anatomist of the soul. We injure thereby that delicacy of perception, so essential to one who has to understand the minute beauties of God's revelation. It is possible to renew, to get back—this is what David asks for—until we get nearer and nearer to innocency,

> "And with the morn those angel-faces smile,
> Which I have loved long since and lost awhile."

A desire for right things, a cleansed inclination, a fresh disposition,—it is a real gift of God, after the tricks we have played with our affection, after the imperfect things we have followed and loved, after the clouding of the fresh impressions of our heavenly origin. "Renew a right spirit within me."

III.

And as he has implored the patience of God and asked for restoration, so now further he asks for the comforts of religion. "Cast me not away from Thy presence: and take not Thy Holy Spirit from me. O give me the comfort of Thy help again: and stablish me with Thy free Spirit."

"The comfort of Thy help." How much there is in these words! It is the great privilege of our profession that we may have such abundant help. Once more our penitence has earned that we may see His face. "Blessed are the pure in heart: for they shall see God."[1] Once more we may look for His guidance, in the cloudy pillar and the leading fire. Once more we may look for the ark coming out of the land of the Philistines. It is a great thing to be supported by a help which is supernatural, not of this world. It is a great thing to be busied in a profession wherein the service of God is the main duty of life, not a mere πάρεργον snatched out of a busy whirl of engrossing care. It is a great thing to be driven, as it were, by the very call of service into the inner presence and glory of God. And the firmness, the stability of the free Spirit, will day by day make us stronger. That Spirit which makes us free; that Spirit which is poured upon us, in a free and full measure. The fruits may be ours, the gifts may be ours, the inner life may be ours. What a difference now to the prodigal asking for pity and pardon! Where is the offence, the sin, the wickedness, the fault, now? Comfort, stability, pardon, and peace meet us in their place. Certainly we must try and rise upon our dead selves to greater

---

[1] S. Matt. v. 8.

heights than ever. There it is; there is my life! Shall I leave it in ruins, and hopelessly try to cut myself off from it? Or shall I pull down in penitence all that is amiss, restore, rebuild, renew, by God's grace, and out of it make a temple meet for Him, stablished by His free Spirit? "Let Thy hand be upon the man of Thy right hand: and upon the son of man, whom Thou madest so strong for Thine own self."[1]

[1] Ps. lxxx. 17.

IV.

"Then shall I teach Thy ways unto the wicked: and sinners shall be converted unto Thee. Deliver me from blood-guiltiness, O God, Thou that art the God of my health: and my tongue shall sing of Thy righteousness. Thou shalt open my lips, O Lord: and my mouth shall shew Thy praise. For Thou desirest no sacrifice, else would I give it Thee: but Thou delightest not in burnt offerings. The sacrifice of God is a troubled spirit: a broken and contrite heart, O God, shalt Thou not despise."—Ps. li. 13-17.

WE are now close on Mid-Lent Sunday. Lent is half gone. Are we satisfied? Have we done what we meant to do; given up what we hoped to give up; made good what we determined to rectify? Do not let us be disheartened. Just as sometimes, owing to our weakness, we have missed, through our wandering thoughts, all the petitions of a collect, and then, recollecting ourselves, have thrown all our energy into the concluding "Amen," and have hoped and believed that the virtue of the prayer has not all been lost to us, so let us make what remains of Lent the earnest "Amen," as it were, to an imperfect devotion, and, by our concentration on what remains, try and recover what is lost.

In these verses the psalm seems to take now a brighter turn. There is a mention of teaching, of a service of praise, of a sacrifice, as if the poor, crushed spiritual life were gaining strength again. Just as when a man is recovering from a serious illness, the very fact of his becoming impatient is a good sign. So here David is becoming impatient, as it were, of his low condition; he is thinking of work, he is making plans. And, indeed, it has been a very sad spectacle. We saw first the poor broken, shattered soul, with God outraged, self-respect gone, spiritual life injured, character broken, and the poison of sin admitted. Then there was the great "I absolve thee," the washing, the whitening, the repairing of the injury; and then there was the restoration to something like what he was before, by the help of the princely Spirit. Now there is a higher hope still. His sin, his fall, his penitence, may become a source of actual spiritual strength. "Many shall see it, and fear: and shall put their trust in the Lord."[1] David's pardon, David's restoration, shall be the great ground of hope and conversion for generations of penitents. It is a grand idea to utilize faults. God can do it. We have read of the painter who, in his rage and disappointment at not being able to represent the foam on the mouth of a Fury, threw his sponge at the picture, and so produced without design the effect for which he had laboured. But God can take our very faults and beautify them, as an architect seizes upon an uneven site as the opportunity for fresh picturesqueness of detail to his building. So that it has been said, the three great doctors of the Catholic Church are David the murderer, S. Peter the denier, and S. Paul the persecutor: "Though he fall, he shall not be cast away: for the Lord upholdeth him with His hand."[2]

I.

"Then shall I teach." We all hope to do something more than save our own souls. We are here for this very purpose, to train ourselves that we may help others. Let

---

[1] Ps. xl. 4.   [2] Ps. xxxvii. 24.

us recognize this important truth then, at once—that our teaching will be of no avail, that no converting will be possible, without penitence.

Do not let us begin the psalm at ver. 13. In the word "then" we have a great truth. It may be that we are laying now, in this Lent, the real foundation of our teaching-life; preparing for those powers of conversion with which God may bless us. For, after all, it is not cleverness, nor powers of preaching, nor great resource of learning, nor logical acuteness, nor skilful fence, nor knowledge of men and things, which is the main requisite. It is the heart, the clean heart; the heart which is swept by the Holy Spirit. A message from those words of mysterious depth penetrates here too. "For their sakes I sanctify Myself."[1] Do we not owe it to the people that our hearts shall be quite clean; that we should not give them to eat of pastures which we have trampled down, nor to drink of waters which become foul as they wash past us, and so for our sakes men abhor the offering of the Lord? Remember we are the burning-glasses which concentrate the

[1] S. John xvii. 19.

rays of the sun on some heart: what if we are dusty and defiled? Remember we have the terrible responsibility of delivering the Lord's message: what if we have been incapacitated for receiving it at God's hands? "He did not many mighty works there because of their unbelief."[1] Is that the reason why we say we shall not offer our people the blessing of Daily Service, because we have not overcome the old habits of spiritual indolence; because we have never valued it ourselves; because we have so seldom made the effort to pass through the penitential barrier, and mount the steps of prayer and praise? Is that the reason why we shall give them so seldom the privilege of an early Celebration, because we have not got over some habit of laziness? Is this sometimes also the reason why priests never go to their schools, and leave to neglect, or the popular religion of the day—"undenominationalism"—the precious souls of the young generation, the new blood of the Church? Is this the reason why our sermons are so dull and pointless, because we have not broken through habits of prayerlessness?

[1]. S. Matt. xiii. 58.

Is this the reason why the inhabitants of towns and villages are unvisited, because we have not yet learned the value of a soul? Is this the reason why, when some poor wretched, afflicted sinner comes to us, bowed down by sin, we say, "My good friend, we must have no one between us and God;" because perhaps we have never tasted the awful bitterness, the healing smart of penitence? And there are some people to whom the penitent would find it nearly impossible to make a confession.

It is a great fact that the key which unlocks the mysteries of God is, in many senses, a moral one. "If any man will do His will, he shall know of the doctrine, whether it be of God."[1] It is only too possible to wish some doctrines not to be true; it is perfectly impossible to understand many of them from the outside. And, therefore, let this Lent be, for all of us, the very foundation of our teaching power. "Then shall I teach."

It is thus we learn sympathy. Ah, here is a poor soul going through all which I have gone through: "I too was a stranger in the

[1] S. John vii. 17.

land of Egypt." It is thus we acquire tenderness: "For we ourselves also were sometimes foolish, disobedient, deceived, serving divers lusts and pleasures, living in malice and envy, hateful, and hating one another."[1] It is thus that we acquire spiritual might. "If God so loved us," says the Apostle of love, "we ought also to love one another."[2] Do we yet know how God loves us? Have we been caught up on high? Have we looked out on the world from His bosom? Do we really know what a Communion is, apart from all the weariness of controversy? "My beloved is mine, and I am His."[3] Do we know what conviction is, after the pain of doubt? "Thomas answered and said unto Him, My Lord and my God."[4] Do we know what gratitude is? "Tell me therefore, which of them will love Him most? ... I suppose that he, to whom He forgave most."[5] Conviction is the teacher's storehouse, earnestness is the instrument of conversion; but they both imply the first twelve verses of this psalm, and are introduced by this word "Then."

[1] Titus iii. 3. [2] 1 S. John iv. 11.
[3] Cant. ii. 16. [4] S. John xx. 28. [5] S. Luke vii. 42, 43.

II.

"And my tongue shall sing of Thy righteousness . . . my mouth shall shew Thy praise." He is talking of service—David, the blood-stained adulterer. But here, too, again it runs, "Deliver me from blood-guiltiness"—"and" or "then." So that we have another application of the same truth: penitence this Lent is our preparation for the life of service in the sanctuary. Our people do not come to church—they like the meeting-house better; or they are cold and indifferent spectators if they do come? Why is it? Sometimes, if we must speak the truth, services are terribly perfunctory, cold, and slovenly. We clergy are in constant danger of deterioration. There is no doubt whatever that you are taking upon yourselves a great strain in the mere conducting of the service. What a tremendous thing is the Daily Eucharist! It may be, "And thou, Capernaum, which art exalted to heaven, shalt be thrust down to hell."[1] What a solemn thing is even the Daily Office, bring-

[1] S. Luke x. 15.

Devotion the Atmosphere of our Lives. 47

ing us into the presence of God! What a call upon us there is to live always in an atmosphere of prayer, if we know that we may be summoned at any moment to a death-bed, there to come close to the very opening gates of Paradise, or to administer the Viaticum to the traveller now almost departing. Is not all this something to be prepared for? We learn to sing the service, how to read the details of the history of what we are saying. Ought we not to be learning how to offer? Here, again, the preparation is a moral or a spiritual one. "Deliver me from blood-guiltiness, O God, *and* my tongue shall sing." If we have a distaste for or a shrinking from these things now, is it because as yet we have never learned their meaning nor heard their grandeur? "It is humiliating to be told that a thing is very fine, when we don't feel it fine. Something like being blind, when people talk of the sky."

> "Look how the floor of heaven
> Is thick inlaid with patines of bright gold.
> There's not the smallest orb which thou behold'st
> But in his motion like an angel sings, . . .
> Such harmony is in immortal souls :
> But whilst this muddy vesture of decay
> Doth grossly close it in, we cannot hear it."

Would not the service have a new meaning to us if it were all a reality?

Our prayers and praises have to reach, not only men, but God. And the true melody of our praises will be that of a good and true life. It just makes all the difference. We may learn this Lent to say the service with pathos, with expression, with fervour; again it is the fervour which has been breathed into it by the first twelve verses of this psalm.

III.

For Thou desirest no sacrifice, else would I give it Thee. . . . The sacrifice of God is a troubled spirit." We are preparing once more this Lent for the service of our lives. After all, there is nothing more powerful than the life of sacrifice. Just the troubled spirit, ruffled, freshened as it were every day by the breath from on high, as in the lovely description of daybreak on the lake—

> "Mildly and soft the western breeze
> Just kissed the lake, just stirred the trees;
> And the pleased lake, like maiden coy,
> Trembled, but dimpled not for joy."

Where the heart is sensitive to every heavenly influence; where the broken heart is full of affection towards God, while it always remembers the past; where the contrite heart is softened, bruised, pulverized into good receptive soil. May we not learn here, too, to offer a sacrifice like this? Have we learned yet to sacrifice inclination? It takes a long time to do this. Père Lacordaire tells us how, in spite of all his austerities, practised with a view of subduing the will, he took a long time before he could overcome his irritation at such a simple thing as being interrupted. Can we give up inclination deliberately? When the summons comes, "Go unto the way that goeth down from Jerusalem unto Gaza, which is desert,"[1] can we go? When we are forbidden of the Holy Ghost to preach the Word in Asia,[2] can we acquiesce? Can we bear all the breaking in upon our meals; Nicodemus coming by night; the crowds coming with their sick, when we want to go up into the mountain? And yet it might be learned here. "Verily, verily, I say unto thee, When thou wast young, thou girdedst thyself, and walkedst whither thou wouldest: but when

[1] Acts viii. 26.   [2] Acts xvi. 6.

thou shalt be old, . . . another shall gird thee, and carry thee whither thou wouldest not."[1] If, as priests, we have to give up our inclination, God might still take it from us as laymen, perhaps no longer a sacrifice but a loss.

Can we give up to God, place at His disposal, our talents—what the world calls "condescend"? A disappointed man is a melancholy spectacle. Why should we be disappointed? If we could only put ourselves unreservedly in God's hands, we should never be disappointed. Mr. Keble was never promoted to any high dignity in the Church, and yet his name will live on through many generations, and his work longer still. Above all, can we part with the besetting sin, fault, weakness, whatever it may be, in the sense of bearing all that is to eradicate it?

"The troubled spirit." We naturally shrink from trouble. "Oh, I cannot. Nathan has no business to talk to me like that! God does not require this anguish from me." But let us remember, "Be not ashamed when it concerneth thy soul. For there is a shame that bringeth sin, and there is a shame which is glory and grace."[2] Then there is the broken

[1] S. John xxi. 18.   [2] Ecclus. iv. 20, 21.

heart, broken in the life-burden which God may be obliged to put upon us. "The sword shall never depart from thine house."[1] And, further, there is the contrite heart, shown in the life of self-denial, patience, gentleness, and submission in which we render to God the sacrifice of our whole being. All these things are professional secrets to learn here during this Lent, in this its most solemn part. We wish to teach, to convert, to sing, to praise, to live the life of sacrifice. Very well. Let us mark the little word "then." It links it all back to the first penitential outburst of the psalm. This Lent is not a concession to an ecclesiastical superstition; it is an integral part, rather it is the foundation, of our future ministerial lives.

[1] 2 Sam. xii. 10.

V.

"O be favourable and gracious unto Sion: build Thou the walls of Jerusalem."—Ps. li. 18.

WITH the idea of teaching, of praising, of a living sacrifice fresh upon him, remembering what he wishes to do, and remembering what one sin has been to him, in its guilt, its consequences, and its terrors—thinking of all this, David seems now to be praying that there may be some greater protection, some more abiding sanctuary of strength, some more firm bulwark of refuge, than he had ever known. Just as before now some traveller, who has found his way on a foggy night to the bridge across the river by the sound of the church bells, which indicated to him his course; has in consequence, to show his gratitude, left to posterity an endowment for ringing the bells to warn belated wanderers; or as a sick man, who by God's help has been restored unexpectedly to health, leaves provision for a bed in a hospital as a thank-offering; so David here seems anxiously to search about for some greater protection for the poor sons of Adam, the prey of passion and the sport of temptation, to which he could point them. So that he has been thought in these verses to pray for, to anticipate, to foresee the rise of the Catholic Church, the great mountain of safety, the bulwark against the spiritual foes of man—Sion established in favour and grace; Jerusalem built up with encircling walls, the glory of God and the salvation of men. "O be favourable and gracious unto Sion: build Thou the walls of Jerusalem."

Now, there is a traditional interpretation of these two terms. Sion is the Church militant here on earth; Jerusalem, the vision of peace, is the Church triumphant,[1] the Church in heaven. So we read, "That they may declare the name of the Lord in Sion, and His worship at Jerusalem; when the people are gathered together, and the kingdoms also, to serve the Lord."[2] His name in the earthly

---

[1] See Dr. Neale, "Psalms," dissertation iii., vol. i. pp. 434-436.
[2] Ps. cii. 21.

Sion now; His worship in the heavenly Jerusalem hereafter, where the ransomed and elect people of the saints shall be gathered together, when "the kingdoms of this world are become the kingdoms of our Lord, and of His Christ."[1] If this be so, his prayer has been wonderfully answered. God has indeed been favourable and gracious unto Sion; a fountain is opened to the house of David and to the inhabitants of Jerusalem for sin and for uncleanness,[2] in the Holy Church. The awful presence of God has passed into the living Sacramental Presence of Christ, to give strength and joy, symbolized by the bread and wine. Here there is no sacrifice of the blood of bulls and goats, which can never take away sin, but the one great Sacrifice for sins for ever. Here God the Father meets His people; here God our Advocate helps them, whose sins would for ever have shut them out; here God the Holy Spirit broods over the waters of Baptism, or troubles the blood-red pool of Absolution, or strengthens the hand of Confirmation, or is present to consecrate the Eucharist, or intercedes in His people with groanings which cannot be

[1] Rev. xi. 15.   [2] Zech. xiii. 1.

uttered.[1] Favour and grace, these are the two distinguishing marks. God has a favour unto us; a rich store of grace is laid up for us; the whole armour of God is waiting for the sorely tried warrior.

And, dear brethren, it is your blessed privilege to be ministers of this favour and grace, to help to build up Sion. It is yours to show people that they need never sin like David, nor fall under temptation.

It may be your lot to be sent to a place where Sion is weak, almost broken down; where the Church has ceased to be a force; where the world, the flesh, and the devil are running riot. What shall you do? Build up Sion. First set up the altar; have a great centre of life in the parish, where God's grace can meet your need. You say that people will not appreciate it, or understand it. Surely they will when they begin to realize what it is.

Then you will go on building up Sion, by the Daily Service. Twice a day, at least, the people will know that you have gone in to intercede for them before God. Then you will go outwards, building up walls as you go.

[1] Rom. viii. 26.

You will build up your choir, and then you will build up your school, and then your Church workers, and then your general body of communicants; and then you will have a sanctuary into which can be drawn, more and more, those who are weak, sinful, and weary, who will find the Church a refuge, the shadow of a great rock in a weary land.[1]

Or it may be your lot to go to a place where there is Church-life in appearance, but not in reality; where there are Eucharists, and people do not come; Daily Services which are unappreciated; an empty church, and cold formalism. What a temptation then it will be to throw it all up; to launch out into some new effervescence, or to have perpetual missions, or fanatical preaching; to give away this or that doctrine as a sop to unpopularity; to throw out to them the Creeds, or Inspiration, or the Sacraments. But this is not Sion. Remember, men cannot live on excitement—they want meat; and also that faith is one great surrender, not the sum-total of acceptance of a string of doctrines, which have been tapped and tested every one, to see if they will bear the pro-

[1] Isa. xxxii. 2.

digious weight of human intellect and critical acumen.

And surely now is the time in which to learn what Sion is, what it means, what it can be, what it shall be.

What is the Holy Eucharist to you now? It will be the same to the struggling masses to whom you hope to give it. What is the Daily Service to you now? If it helps you, it can equally help all. What is Absolution to you now? If it helps you against sin, it equally helps others. What is the Prayer-book, the Church system in its fulness? Is it a reality?

What a difference it makes, if a man knows how to act in an emergency! A house which had been furnished with every appliance against fire was, not so long ago, burned down, because the servants had not been instructed in the use of the different methods for extinguishing the flames. Sion may be there, all furnished and fortified, and yet fail to be a help, because we its servants do not know how to man it, or make it servicable. "O be favourable and gracious unto Sion." If we could only make men see the force, the power, the beauty of

Church principles, then David's prayer would be abundantly answered. It sometimes seems to succeed, just to touch the surface of men's needs. But it does not answer in the end. It is not Sion.

II.

"Build Thou the walls of Jerusalem." As Sion gains in strength, so these walls of Jerusalem begin to rise. In proportion as our blessed Lord helps forward His earthly Church, in the same degree does He build the walls of Jerusalem above. "Jerusalem shall be built up with sapphires, and emeralds, and precious stone: thy walls and towers and battlements, with pure gold. And the streets of Jerusalem shall be paved with beryl, and carbuncle, and stones of Ophir. And all her streets shall say, Alleluia."[1]

> "Jerusalem, Jerusalem!
>   God grant that I may see
> Thy endless joys, and of the same
>   Partaker aye may be.
> Thy walls are made of precious stone,
>   Thy bulwarks diamonds square;
> Thy gates are of right orient pearl,
>   Exceeding rich and rare;

---

[1] Tobit xiii. 16-18.

> Thy turrets and thy pinnacles
>   With carbuncles do shine;
> Thy very streets are paved with gold,
>   Surpassing rich and fine;
> Thy houses are of ivory,
>   Thy windows crystal clear,
> Thy tiles are made of beaten gold;—
>   O God, that I were there!"

You remember, when the temple was being built of old, that it was built of stone made ready before it came there. "So that there was neither hammer nor axe nor any tool of iron heard in the house, while it was in building."[1] Do you realize how silently and slowly that Jerusalem above is now being raised? There are stones being prepared for it in the crowded streets of the city, cut out amidst all the temptation, distraction, and worry of a hard life. In the hospital there is being shaped out some ruby, by sharp suffering. Right away in the heart of Africa there are stones being prepared, timber being cut. In some quiet village, where life seems to stagnate, there are the plates of beaten gold being finished. And this is what we have to superintend. Are we ready for it; are we willing to do it? It sometimes

[1] 1 Kings vi. 7.

seems rather dull and monotonous, simply to get ready a few rough stones, to smooth them and polish them. It sometimes seems as if we were working for no purpose, where we do not know the plan; we should rather be where the work was of a more delicate kind, or nearer completion. We should rather be carving capitals or handling metal and precious stones. But Jerusalem has to be built. It is a solemn thought that there are some stones waiting for us. The block of marble so cold and shapeless is waiting for its Michael Angelo to let the angel out of it. Is there, think you, some soul, now blinded and stunned, who has lost his way, and who is waiting for you to be an Ananias to him, to rise from your prayers and go and lay your hands on him that he may see? Is there some Onesimus, some runaway slave, who has waited on you, perhaps, at dinner, and heard your conversation, and felt drawn to you, and now is waiting for you to come to the great city, that he may find you out, and get you to restore him to honesty and to usefulness—to be a S. Paul to him? Is there any S. Mark, who has failed, who has gone back, and whose life is trembling in the scale, who is waiting just for your sympathy and help to give him another chance—to be a S. Barnabas to him? Is there any Apollos, who is waiting for you to teach him the way of God more perfectly? Ah! is there any Saul waiting for your martyrdom? "Thy martyr Stephen."[1] He never forgot it, the patient angel-face of that holy man, lifted up into the vision of Jesus Christ, at the right hand of God, before the stones yet severed the bands which kept him down to earth. Martyrdom may even now be the lot of those who build up Jerusalem. Mr. Lowder commenced his life and work of devoted usefulness at S. Peter's, London Docks, amidst the howling of mobs, and threats and execrations; at the last his dead body was followed by a weeping parish, who had lost their best friend. There are towns and villages waiting for you—Sodom, which you may save by the lives of yourself and household; tossed and anxious mariners on life's sea, whom God will give to your prayers. But what if, when we reach our appointed task, we sink back powerless because we do not know our methods, and have no consciousness of our

[1] Acts xxii. 20.

powers? See, then, the vast importance of this Lent. We are learning now to build up Jerusalem. It is heart-work, it is soul-work; it is learned on the knees, it is learned at the foot of the cross, it is learned in the contemplation of your meditation, it is learned at the altar. The wall of the city is waiting for me. There are souls being cast away for want of help. There are precious stones which will never be built in.

III.

Once more we stop to listen to those mysterious words, "For their sakes I sanctify Myself."[1] A great deal depends on our own personal equipment for the task before us. Sion and Jerusalem, these are the two aims which we must put before us. It means labour; have we faced that? "We then, as workers together with Him,"[2] must expect to labour in carrying out His work. It means that the Samaritans will come and hinder us; have we faced that? "Let there be no temple at all," they say, "if not in our way, and with every concession to our

---
[1] S. John xvii. 19.   [2] 2 Cor. vi. 1.

prejudices." It means failure. It is told of a preacher returning from a great religious meeting that, seeing a man terribly intoxicated, he remarked to a friend, "Do you see that man? He is one of my converts." His friend expressing surprise at the remark, he further added, "Yes, mine, but not God's." It means disappointment, but it also means lasting joy. To be a conscious worker with God, should leave absolutely nothing to be desired. God grant that this Passion-tide may see us girding ourselves anew for the task!

Sion, let that represent to us Church principles; Jerusalem, let that be to us earnest work in the salvation of men's souls.

VI.

"Then shalt Thou be pleased with the sacrifice of righteousness, with the burnt offerings and oblations: then shall they offer young bullocks upon Thine altar."—Ps. li. 19.

THE first impulse of a generous soul, when he sees the ruin, the desolation, the broken wall, and the gaps of sin, is to offer reparation, to make restitution, to restore, to do something to make good the desolating ravages of sin. "He shall restore the lamb fourfold, because he did this thing, and because he had no pity."[1]

Alas! this is not always possible. Mummius, the Roman general to whose lot it fell to sack Corinth, with all its treasures of art and monuments of antiquity, is said to have told his rough soldiers that if they broke any of these works of art they would have to replace them. Perhaps his is not a less ludicrous conception who thinks to repair the

[1] 2 Sam. xii. 6.

ravages of sin. Innocency was a work of art which came right from the hand of God. Penitence, after all, is but an indifferent copy, which has lost the living colour and the delicate bloom of God's own inspiration. What can I do with all these broken fragments, these failures, these negligences, these ignorances? Just think what I might have been, if I had only read diligently all through the days of my early training, instead of squandering time and opportunities in idleness; if all the prayers I had put up had been real prayers; if there had not been all those yawning gaps and fissures in my life! Think of all the lives that have crossed mine: have they got good or harm? Yes, indeed, if only we had the power we would gladly restore, repair, make up for the past.

And it is just here that David seems to look forward, not only to a more perfect contrition, a more prevailing confession, but also to a more acceptable satisfaction for sin. The sacrifice of righteousness of One Who is righteous, of One Who makes righteous, of One Who accounts righteous. The sacrifice of Calvary, in the Sion of the Church, in the Jerusalem above,—in this, and by this alone, will it be possible to repair, to restore, to make God again well pleased, by virtue of the atonement of His dear Son.

It has that wonderful power, as we have seen, of weaving all our life together. Where the great tower fell in pride, there is a fresh beauty rising up in humility. All the different failures, incongruities, half-beginnings, impulses, longings of our life, are brought together, in some marvellous way, by His master hand; our very sins have been seized upon, to strengthen or beautify, or even tone down, our life. " In heaven I shall be myself." Tenderness, gentleness, self-distrust, and many delicate virtues like them, have been brought into our lives, in places where once were ruinous gaps. Truly God is very merciful! Who but He could ever have made life righteous? And we can even reach out after others, by virtue of this sacrifice. We feel and know that in the Holy Eucharist, the perpetual memorial of the sacrifice, we can intercede, we can stand before God and plead; we can ask Him to find out and bring back those whom our carelessness or sin may have injured.

David's fall and David's penitence, they

are wonderfully balanced in their effect by the power of Almighty God. And that which David so looked forward to we are just about again to put before us, that we may contemplate it, analyze it, pray over it, test its virtue, bring it into our life, use it—the great sacrifice of righteousness, which is the object of the coming Holy Week. To have a fixed time like this in which to consider so great a mystery, is a very great privilege. Just as when you want to look at a flower under the microscope, you know that if you put the whole blossom beneath the magnifying lens, you will see nothing, only a blur of red, or a blur of blue, as the case may be; but, if you take it to pieces and put a leaf, or a piece of a leaf, or the tiniest fragment, before you, then you see its beauty and its organism, its delicacy, and its completeness; so with the great facts of our Redemption. If we look at them all at once, the subject is too vast; it confuses, it dazzles; we see nothing. But during this Holy Week we are trying to disengage just this blood-red blossom of the Atonement, and to look at it piece by piece, tenderly, lovingly, prayerfully; this sacrifice of righteousness; now turning full upon it the strong light of Old Testament prophecy, now approaching it with the long sustained gaze of prayer, or the elevating aspiration of praise. The Blessed Mother invites us there, to join in love with her for the dearest, the closest friend; S. John invites us to look at mysteries; "the other Mary," that we may see the secret of a quiet life of benevolence; S. Mary Magdalene invites all who have experienced a great deliverance; the penitent thief all who are suffering for sin. "Come and learn, come and see. Here is the sacrifice of righteousness, with which God is well pleased."

And yet we would not stay here; we would not say in a helpless, aimless way, "I believe that Jesus died for me."

The prayer of the generous heart in all ages is to be "made conformable unto His death;"[1] to reproduce, however faintly, the pangs, the afflictions, the generous self-sacrifice, the agony of Gethsemane, the shame of Calvary; to offer in person to God a sacrifice of righteousness, righteous because in union with Him, righteous because sprinkled with His blood, righteous because it is the

[1] Phil. iii. 10.

best which we can offer. And it is here described.

I.

First of all, there will be the burnt offering. You know what that means. It is that sacrifice where all is burned and consumed— a type of the complete exhaustion of wrath against sin.[1] It must be taken from the herd and from the flock, things ready to hand, just round about the home, and be killed, flayed, cut into pieces, and burnt. Is not this the sacrifice which we fain would offer, the vengeance on ourselves, the sorrow after a godly sort, with its carefulness, its clearing of ourselves, its indignation, its fear, its vehement desire, its zeal, its revenge?[2] Killed, flayed, cut into pieces, and burnt,—can we do this? Are we dead to the old temptation, are we mortified? We know how, in the stern rites of profession in the Religious orders, everything was designed to show a death unto the world. So we must be dead to the old temptation, that is, like a dead man in the presence of sin and its old allurements; we

---

[1] See Bonar, "Leviticus," chap. i. pp. 11, 12.
[2] 2 Cor. viii. 11.

must flay the sinful life, lay it bare of all the coverings which we have put upon it. We must burn it, consume it with the fire of repentance, with the hatred of a vengeance, with the love of God. God grant that this week may see in us our sins killed, flayed, and burnt; our whole selves a living sacrifice, acceptable unto God; dead to sin, stripped of all which hides us from Him, burnt and consumed with His love.

II.

But he goes on to look for *the oblation*, the peace offering—that offering which the soul can make when it is at peace with God. Ours is to be the life of oblation, the life in which there is the perpetual offering up of self. This, too, is a lesson to learn on Calvary, to offer ourselves to God, and to whatever work He may give us to do. When the servant of Abraham took his journey to find a wife for his master's son, he stood by the well to wait and see whether God would send him the object of his search.[1] We too must give ourselves up to stand and wait for those whom God will send to us, those to whom we have

---

[1] Gen. xxiv.

a special mission out of the busy throng who pass by us.

Here is one coming to consult you, because he believes that you have studied and have thought, and are instructed; can you offer yourself to the lonely watch-tower, where you can observe, study, and compare, and receive at the hand of God the instruction which will help you to deal with the needs of a man's soul? Or here is one coming to you in the despair of an overmastering temptation; can you offer yourself now to God, in all the pureness, patience, and self-discipline which is necessary if you would study the phenomena of sin, so as to be able to relieve it with gentleness, tenderness, and skill? Here are many preparing themselves to come to your ministrations; can you offer yourself to God, that you may learn how to stand before Him, how to swing the censer of prayer, how to plead the sacrifice, to praise, to pray? It is on Calvary that we learn the dedicated life.

III.

But he goes higher still. Young bullocks will be offered on the altar. This means the best and the costliest offering. The bullock was the offering for the priest—the most bulky, the most expensive form of sacrifice that could be got. The priest had to offer the very same kind of sacrifice as when the whole congregation had sinned.[1] It is the sacrifice of a life which God demands from the priest. It is the sacrifice of a life which God asks us to contemplate on Calvary. "Be ye therefore perfect."[2] Is this an idle dream? He was perfect. "Which of you convinceth Me of sin?"[3] He asks, without fear of the answer. Can we be perfect too? At least, we are bound to try. We can make a resolution never to put up with that which is imperfect, whether it be something which we shrink back from, beaten and hopeless, saying, "I cannot attain unto it;" whether it be some disposition or some habit, whose attainment ever eludes it ; whether it be those little traits of Christianity, which more than anything else give the likeness to the ideal, which we are seeking to reproduce. We must never rest until we have attained at least this

---

[1] Bonar, "Leviticus," chap. iv. p. 65.
[2] S. Matt. v. 48. [3] S. John viii. 46.

measure of perfection, which is never satisfied with anything short of the highest.

Another contribution to perfection would be, to recognize that it is the evenness of Christ's life which is so beautiful; that He was in all circumstances, and under every trial, always the same, perfect God; and so to make our lives as priests more lives of even holiness, with less of those abrupt intervals and sharp divisions which we have already noticed.

And then to recognize in Him, the source of His perfection, as being the union of the manhood with the Godhead; mysteriously revealed in the strength and peace of the quiet mountain-top, and the communings with the Father. So we, too, as priests, have our times of quiet and of prayer; and one occupation of this Holy Week, which would stand us in good stead, would be to learn to be alone.

Do not let us shrink from this. This is the sacrifice of the young bullock, the sacrifice of a life, which aims at perfection. The priest must combine in himself all the virtues of his congregation; if they are his superiors in many other things, they must not be his superiors in holiness. Surely this Holy Week may be a very precious time to us all ; here are lessons which we shall all do well to gather. " He that hath ears to hear, let him hear."

Looking back over a ministerial life with all its failures, one can but long that you may start out with all the words of this psalm vibrating as it were within you. Grieved at the imperfection of the past, yet confident for the future ; sorry, contrite, pardoned, at peace ; with the manful penitence of a devoted life, and the free-will sacrifice of all your being, caught up at last into the *Gloria Patri, et Filio, et Spiritui Sancto* of heaven.

PEACE

Psalm XXIII.

"Neque ut dominantes in cleris, sed forma facti gregis ex animo. Et cum apparuerit princeps pastorum, percipietis immarescibilem gloriæ coronam."

I.

"The Lord is my Shepherd; I shall not want."—Ps. xxiii. 1.

THERE is almost a profanation in expanding a psalm like this, where to touch may mean to destroy, and to expand only to dilute; and yet Holy Scripture, being all golden, submits, as no other writings can, to analysis and minute treatment without any sacrifice of its value, and to constant drawings off of its rich support and vigorous joy without any appreciable diminution of its strength. Here we can see the shepherd arguing from out of his own experience and the humble occupations of his youth; from the care that he felt for the sheep committed to his charge, to the greater love and greater care which God Almighty shows for the sheep of His pasture, the frail and erring children of men. As he sees the sunset reddening the sky, as he hears the howl of some beast of prey, he feels that his sheep are safe; he knows how to defend them. As he sees the green pastures beneath him, and notes the silver sheets of still water, like "the eyes of the landscape;" as he sees the mist curling in the valley, with a growing chill and gloom on the edge of the advancing night, he knows of other pastures, he thinks of another valley. "The Lord is my Shepherd; I shall not want. . . . Yea, though I walk through the valley of the shadow of death, I will fear no evil: for Thou art with me; Thy rod and Thy staff they comfort me."

Surely experience of this kind is a very blessed thing. It is, after all, our ultimate book of reference. "Now we believe, not because of thy saying: for we have heard Him ourselves, and know that this is indeed the Christ, the Saviour of the world."[1] We should cherish our experience almost as a second volume of Holy Scriptures; it should be to us, all that memory has been said to be, of which the novelist has written, "His memory was a volume where *vide supra* could serve instead of repetition, and not the ordi-

---

[1] S. John iv. 42.

nary long-used blotting-book, which only tells of forgotten writing."

I.

These words of the psalmist Jesus Christ has, as it were, made His own. "I am the good Shepherd." He has expounded them in that discourse which S. John has recorded for us, when He was dealing with the case of the poor blind man now restored to sight, but expelled from the synagogue by an unreasoning fanaticism;[1] and if we would understand the full meaning of this verse, we should carefully examine that passage in the Evangelist.

It has been pointed out[2] that it contains three allegories or similitudes. In the first, our blessed Lord says that He is like the true shepherd, who comes to lead his sheep out in the early morning from the high enclosure in which they had been kept during the night, mixed with other flocks, under the charge of one man, called the porter. He comes, like the true shepherd, to the door to claim His sheep; the porter knows Him, the

[1] S. John ix.
[2] Dr. Liddon, "Easter Sermons," vol. ii., Serm. xxvii.

sheep recognize Him. He goes before His sheep, who, hearing His voice, follow Him as He leads them into the green pastures. This is the first allegory.

In the second, it is midday, when the sun is scorching with its full power; and here Jesus Christ says He is like the door of an enclosure, a field shelter, through which the sheep stray in and out and find pasture.

In the third allegory, it is evening. As He is leading the flock back to the enclosure, the wolf comes, and, in defending His sheep, the good Shepherd lays down His life for them.

There now stands out clearly, under the illuminating light of the Gospel, a full meaning to this verse which it never had before. "The Lord is my Shepherd; I shall not want;" for He will guard me against three certain causes of want—aimlessness in life; exposure to the world; and, above all, sin.

II.

1. First of all, then, Jesus Christ comes to me, with His shepherd's care, to give me an aim or an object in life. Morning by morning He approaches those who have charge

of us, whoever they may be—home life with all its pressing duties, business life with all its engrossing cares, pleasure with all its wayward forgetfulness—and claims us: "That sheep is Mine." There is no place, or business, or occupation which is free from the obligations of religion, where His claim upon us does not reach. Neither is it only in view of the one great aim in life to which He is gradually drawing us on. It is not that, wander as we will, stop as we will, even lie down, still He is gradually drawing us on to a point. It is more than this. He helps us to have an aim in each day. It dawns upon us increasingly as time slips by, that there is a great danger of losing whole days out of life, whose very seconds are of gold. The day before something, or the day after something, when we dream in prospect, or stay ourselves on retrospect. There is the same danger in holiday-time, after a hard spell of work, after an examination, after some summit reached or some corner turned. We have felt it as children; we have felt it as we grew older, under the strain of effort. "In a fortnight's time life will be life indeed!" or "Next week," or "To-morrow." But the good

G

Shepherd brings us back to "to-day." Life is too short, too valuable, absolutely to miss an hour; but it requires nothing short of the grace of God to get the particular good out of each day—to do just the day's work, to make just the day's spiritual observations as they flit across the *templum*[1] of our vision. We shall never see this particular day of the week, month, and year in combination again. There have been different combinations to-day of trial, temptation, service, grace, manifestations of God, which will never occur again in the same way. This day will reappear somewhere, in the finished work of our life, if it be but a speck, a dash of colour, a twist of character, the slightest warp. It is a lesson which a priest must learn before he faces the immense privileges, yet terrible temptations, of a country parsonage. It is a lesson which all must learn who have to snatch the prey from the still waters of a quiet life, where one day comes up and is succeeded by another, apparently its exact counterpart, with undeviating regularity, yet each day charged

---

[1] An allusion to the ancient system of auguries, where the augurs would mark off a space in the sky called a *templum*, and take their omens from the birds which flitted across it.

with its especial blessing to the patient observer. Let us think of the great naturalist, waiting for twenty-nine years to reveal their long-drawn pages of single days, in order to verify a scientific process thereby. This is surely what the good Shepherd would say to us, as He lingers by the door of the sheepfold each morning—the value and importance of a single day: "Look upon single days as single lives; there is no difference between a day and an age." I must not live in yesterday in melancholy regret—

"*O mihi præteritos referat si Jupiter annos.*"

I must not live in to-morrow in "the empty happiness" of castle-building; but in to-day, to seize its blessings—"*Ascensiones in corde suo disposuit.*"[1] Each day is a stair on the great ascent which mounts up to the house of God; to miss a step out of life is to miss a lesson, and to miss the graduated experience which makes of death itself only the last step out of life.

Another day of life, another day of health, another day with God, is offered us. And just as you can see the history of the world, in the different geological formations of its

[1] Ps. lxxxiii. 5, Vulgate.

crust; so, if our life was laid bare, we should see the history of our character made plain in the different strata of our growth. God knows what each day has done for us; what fossil virtues lie buried there, what catastrophes have swept across it. Let that gentle pleading Form, as it speaks to the porter, teach us this—to live each day with Christ. It is piteous to hear anywhere the cry, "If only I had lived differently!"

"A sorrow's crown of sorrow is remembering happier things."

Most piteous in those who need each day, with its varying influences, to contribute to the character of the priest of God.

2. But with the best intentions, and the highest aims, and the strongest determination, there is a good deal of wear and tear in life. The fierce midday sun scorches and burns; temptation does not spare us; trials come to us as messages of God's love. And here the good Shepherd sinks for a moment in the background, and Jesus Christ becomes the open Door; He is my Refuge. And perhaps we seldom pause to think how very much we owe to this protection—think only of the warnings which He gives us, which it is the fashion of an indifferent age even to despise. We shrink

from the very sound of hell; or from anything which savours of dogmatic precision. Instead of proclaiming that a right faith is necessary to salvation, we say rather, "Go where you like, and believe what you like, if you are in earnest." But still we must feel that we owe an immense debt of gratitude to the Catholic Creeds. Think only of the waste of energy, the cruel falls and hideous scars which must have awaited us, had we been allowed to stray and wander just where we willed. We feel now that speculation is closed in this direction, and demonstration ceases in that. It is the boundary-line of faith, where the ordinary methods are not current, and in itself this is a strength simply to repose on the greatness and authority of God.

> "Oh, what doubts, what drear negations,
> Straightway 'neath our feet are trod,
> When we answer with our Credo
> In a true and living God!"

And no less should we be grateful for His warnings as to the sharp punishment which awaits sin; often and often we must run in pierced and bleeding, caught by the bristling hedge of the Law, which guards the way against our trespass.

In many ways, some stern, some gentle,

we shall find Him our Refuge. His promises are so bright, as each day He leads us to another pasture, as one day's need is met by one day's bread. See, He implores us to cast away anxiety, and repose in Him, more especially those "sorrows beyond all other sorrows, which never come." His comforts are so real. The Altar with its blessed food meets us, as, like an army crossing the desert, marching from well to well, we go from Communion to Communion in our pilgrimage. The church in our midst, our sanctuary from the pursuing talon of an overmastering temptation, opens its doors to receive us. Sundays greet us as days of light and refreshment, when the air is brighter, and less clouded with the smoke of worldly business. His Word shines out as a lantern unto our feet, and a light unto our paths, as we plunge along refreshed in the midst of trouble. All these open on our path as His shelters and refuges. "Thou art a place to hide me in;" where in the busiest life we can be as hermits, beneath the tree of the Cross, within sound of the water of grace, hidden in the cave of the wounded Side. "Thou shalt hide them privily by Thine own presence from the provoking of all men: Thou shalt keep them secretly in Thy tabernacle from the strife of tongues."[1]

3. But the time comes when the wolf springs. It may be as we are nearing home. Job was settled in life, with all his comforts round him, when Satan obtained permission to try him. S. Peter had almost passed through the trial-time of his training with our blessed Lord when he fell. Moses, again, broke down under his besetting sin quite at the end of his life. To speak with reverence, our blessed Lord was tempted by Satan within three years of the end of His sojourn on earth.[2] We habitually pray in our Burial Service, "Suffer us not, at our last hour, for any pains of death, to fall from Thee." Our temptation, the temptation which is to try us and test us, may be yet to come! But whenever it does come, we shall know what it is to have a good Shepherd, Who lays down His life for the sheep. For it is He Who steps in between us and our sins, by His Sacraments, by sustaining hope, by answer to our prayers. If we fall, still He

[1] Ps. xxxi. 22.
[2] I am indebted to the Bishop of Lincoln for this idea.

does not leave us. Again and again, alas! we commit the same sins; again and again He receives us, most willing to turn again, most willing to pardon.

III.

And to those who seek to be like Him, shepherds of the people, what higher model can be offered?

Cannot we, too, give an aim to our people —claim them for God from their earliest childhood; claim them at school, from the porter, whoever he may be, who keeps them, whether the State, or the parish, or the parents? They are His people and the sheep of His pasture, to whom we can teach the value of life, or at least impart that habit of prayer, which lingers on when so much else has broken away, like the ring in the fairy tale, clinging to the finger, forgotten, disused, but still there in time of need, a safety against death. Then, as the day of life goes on, we may be a shelter to the young men, an open door with Christ in the background, where we can help them with the spiritual powers which He puts into our hands, or give them of our friendship, or cheer them with our sympathy. And then, at the last, we can lay down our life for them, the life of pleasure which so long kept us in thrall, the life of self-pleasing and personal aims, while we devote ourselves to our people, ready to sacrifice even life itself, amidst the fevered alleys, in the poisonous atmosphere of the sick-room.

At least we shall feel this, whatever opportunities of doing good God may give us, " He has been a good Shepherd to me; I will also be a good shepherd to them."

II.

"He maketh me to lie down in green pastures: He leadeth me beside the still waters."—Ps. xxiii. 2.

THE good Shepherd has not exhausted His lovingkindness, by leading us out day by day with an aim and an object for our life. He is more to us than the covert from the heated world; more even than our defence in the day of trouble. This psalm goes on to show us how there are still certain details of life which are so many fresh occasions of mercy and love. For having loved His own which are in the world, He loves them unto the end. Here, then, are certain specific acts of kindness which characterize His shepherd-rule, about which there hangs an atmosphere of repose, peace, and comfort—words which perhaps we cling to more and more as the way gets longer, and the sun hotter, and the road harder and browner.

That the weary may lie down; that the

pastures should be green, and no longer the scanty tufts of grass, bespattered by the dust and trampled by the traffic of the roadside; that the waters should be still, waters which can comfort, waters which can refresh, instead of the scanty rivulet, or the waters fouled by the feet of life's wayfarers;—all this speaks to experience (φωνάντα συνετοῖσι), the greatness of our need being the measure of the sweetness of the promise.

I.

Here is a promise, then, to the weary, of *repose.* Thank God this is not an age of *idleness.* Can we equally say, Thank God this is not an age of repose? It is almost the prevailing stamp which defines the character of the present day—its restlessness. Call it, if you will, impatience; call it hurry. Certainly, whatever is the opposite to repose.

> "We see all sights from pole to pole,
> And glance and rush and bustle by,
> And never once possess our soul
> Before we die."

Certainly the clerical life is more and more becoming a rush, a hurry, an impetuous stream. It breathes through the contempt which is sometimes poured upon the country clergy, as if dwellers in towns were alone in the full current of political or religious life. It is the spirit which impels the stampede away from the villages, towards finishing work rather than foundation work. It characterizes the clerical day. The public duties thronging on the footsteps of each other; the guild meetings, the temperance meetings, the multiplied services; the impatience of old methods, or of long experiments; the absolute grudging of time which is not spent in public work of some marketable value,—all these show how deeply we have tasted of this restless spirit, and that, instead of thirty years at Nazareth and three of ministry, we prefer thirty years before the world and three in the retirement of Nazareth. It is just the same wherever we look. Politics, religion, social movements, are all whirled along, catching up in their gusty flight whatever is on the surface, whatever is light and movable, one scheme sweeping on the dust of another, as if men had imbibed the creed which proclaims, "Whatever is, is wrong, and therefore the opposite to the present system, whatever it is, is right."

But the good Shepherd "maketh me to lie down in green pastures." It has been pointed out by writers on this psalm that we may dwell on the word "green," "the pastures of tender grass," as an indication of freshness and nourishment.

When we remember how everything in life contributes in some way to feed us, and how true it is—

"I am part
Of all that I have seen;"

when we consider, again, how much there is which is brown and withered and trodden under foot, poisonous and foul; it is a promise real and true that the good Shepherd will give us green pastures, as we look to Him for nourishment.

How much there is around us and about us to think of, if only we would be still! The world is eloquent with parables on every side; the walls of our daily environment are hung with pictures. The sower as he sows is also preaching; the lilies as they grow, the ravens as they fly, the fisherman as he plies his trade, the woman as she bakes, the judge as he sits in court,—all are our teachers.

How much there is to observe, as naturalists alone will tell us, to our shame, if we are only patient and ready to watch! And, besides the pastures of our daily experience, there are the deep cool pastures of good books, with a ready supply for our need; above all, there is the Holy Spirit, ever shedding His freshening dew on the daily events of our common life, turning water into wine, and trouble into a cross, and disappointment into a diverted call. We clergy, at all events, must not shut our ears to the cry, now waxing loud and long, that sermons are so thin and so poor. We must not complacently accept the fact, if it be a fact, that so many men stay away altogether from our ministrations. What can we expect, if we never meditate, if we never think, if we never read; if there is no repose and no green pasture, but only such hurried nibbling of roadside verbiage and well-worn platitudes as lie along the dusty track of our daily routine?

If the pastures of God are green because they are fresh, they are also green because they are sheltered. Around them is the protecting hedge of God's Law. God's service is the service of perfect freedom, where to admit any taint of sinfulness is to admit weariness and distastefulness. And, moreover, in and about the pastures, are the trees planted by the water-side, the saints of God, to help us by their examples and shade us by their lives. But, above all, there is the Tree of Life in the midst of the garden, a shelter from the wind, a covert from the tempest, as the shadow of a great rock in a weary land.

Let us try, then, and gain some repose in the midst of this weary restlessness. Repose, if possible, in our methods; for God works slowly, and to work together with Him means to work slowly also. He is *patiens quia æternus.* "You can hurry men, but you cannot hurry God."

Let us gain repose in our daily spiritual life. Restlessness is at the bottom of many hasty actions, which end in flying in the face of God's good providence for us. In our restlessness, we think that even the setting of our spiritual life is wrong; that the Church, our mother who bore us, is not the lady-queen which we thought her to be. The old services are lifeless; ritual or mediævalism, for its own sake, is to revive them. This dies away, soon exhausted, and then new dogmas are necessary to brace up the feeble life; and then all becomes weariness, as formula after formula fails, and, through shame and rebellious egotism, the end is nothingness—a religious blank. So the absence of repose goads a man on, like a mirage in the desert, which promises him the water which he never finds. The restlessness of unsettled belief, the restlessness of no belief, are the punishments which await the neglect of spiritual repose. It is a gust of the storm, which is ever sweeping across the world, in the mystery of its ever-changing fashions; in itself a mystery, in itself a witness that the restless heart is straining after peace in God.

These green pastures are no luxury of religion; they are a necessity of life. Each day must have its Nazareth of devotion, as life has its own Nazareth of subjection in childhood; while to the ministerial life its times of solitude and loneliness may be a Nazareth too—times of refreshment, when He maketh me lie down in the green pastures of living rest.

II.

Another note which rings out clearly in this verse, is peace. "He maketh me to lie down . . . He leadeth me." How sadly the soul needs peace—peace in His felt presence! The world is sown with trouble, but still " He maketh me to lie down . . . He leadeth me."

If we look at that greatest of all troubles, temptation, what a pain and grief it is![1] Just when we are basking in the warm sun of God's love, down comes the buzzing poisonous insect, drawn out, it would seem, by the very sunlight which we are enjoying—powerful, if only to vex; hurtful, if only to annoy; troublous, if only to tease. The very height to which God has brought us, of spiritual, intellectual, or social eminence, seems to encourage it. It preys on our refinement, it haunts our quickened imagination, it rises up out of our deeper study which has disturbed it; the wider our range of penetration, the greater the persistence of its attack. It is then we fall back on His encouraging words, "Fear not; for I am with Thee." It makes all the difference in the world to be taught by Him as to the nature of temptation, Who " was in all points tempted like as we are."[2] It gives

---

[1] See these thoughts amplified in "Sermons for the People," vol. iv., Serm. iv. (S.P.C.K.).
[2] Heb. iv. 15.

fresh strength, to learn from Him that there must be something beyond the poisonous suggestion, namely, the acquiescence which refuses to brush it off; the consent which assimilates the poison. See, further, the very temptation has driven us almost mechanically into ejaculatory prayer. See, we have fallen back on Him; it has made us feel once more that which we were in danger of forgetting—that He is close to us, a very present Help in trouble. And now temptation, the occasion of defeat, has been turned into the opportunity of victory. He has allowed us to fall back upon His presence; He has suffered us thereby to be humbled and proved, and driven out of self-confidence. Panting and affrighted, and doubtful of ourselves, He makes us lie down, He feeds us, He leads us on, where the temptation at one time had seemed likely to kill us.

Nor is temptation the only trouble; over these very green pastures the storm has swept, and the waters have hissed and seethed under the dancing storm-drops. Ah! it was cold and chill when the trees were bending under the blast, "and the dull rain smote us, and the heat thundered within the hills, and the empty pastures were blind with rain." But now the bow of hope and mercy spans the retreating clouds, and the pastures are fresh, and the stream full; meekness, gentleness, brightness, unselfishness, evenness of temper,—all these flowers are coming up out of the earth, saturated with tears and woe. "It is good for me that I have been in trouble: that I may learn Thy statutes."[1] So is it with all the little trials of life. Peace rises out of their furious onslaught, or their petty annoyance. And yet how often little troubles seem to have power to vex and irritate us, even more than great ones!—such things as distraction, interruption, accident, disappointment; so many barriers put in our path to deflect us into duty, so many obstacles to provoke our peevish ill-will. Let us cheerfully recognize that, if the good Shepherd is leading us, there is no such thing as accident. Trifles may very easily interfere with our peace of mind; but they may also be God's messengers to teach us to cast away all appearance of grumbling and fretfulness, and if an obstacle arise in our ministry, to recognize that it is of the Holy Ghost. Or

[1] Ps. cxix. 71.

if our missionary zeal seems quenched in the darkness of a prison, still to be able to write from it the bright message, "Rejoice in the Lord alway;" "I have learned, in whatsoever state I am, therewith to be content."[1] Here is the guardianship of the peace of God, which "passeth all understanding."

III.

And yet there is a third note which swells up in the triple harmony of this verse; and that is, comfort. "In the multitude of the sorrows that I had in my heart: Thy comforts have refreshed my soul."[2] "The waters of quietness" have become in one version of the psalm, which is very dear to us, "the waters of comfort." There is a river which waters Paradise, and it is parted into many heads. Holy Baptism is not something in the dead past, an historical act finished and done with; it is a water which follows us in the new nature of its creating. Grace remains in us from our Confirmation, a store of strength. "He shall dwell on high: his place of defence shall be the munitions of rocks: bread shall be

---

[1] Phil. iv. 4, 11.   [2] Ps. xciv. 19.

given him; his waters shall be sure."[1] Grace remains stored up in Absolution, whenever the angel steps down to trouble the pool. Grace remains in Communion and prayer. "They drank of that spiritual Rock that followed them: and that Rock was Christ."[2] And for us ordained clergy there is the ever-abiding grace which came to us by the imposition of hands. As we pass along our way, led by the good Shepherd in the repose of the green pastures, in the peace of the abiding Presence, in the comfort of the still waters, we can say once more, with a new depth of meaning, "They that are delivered from the noise of archers in the places of drawing water, there shall they rehearse the righteous acts of the Lord, even the righteous acts toward the inhabitants of His villages in Israel."[3]

[1] Isa. xxxiii. 16.   [2] 1 Cor. x. 4.   [3] Judg. v. 11.

III.

"He restoreth my soul: He leadeth me in the paths of righteousness for His Name's sake.—Ps. xxiii. 3.

AFTER the thoughts of repose, peace, and comfort which dominated the last verse, where the refreshing water rippled through the deep, cool grass, making glad the city of God, flowing on to its entrance with the sea, the first word which meets us now is "restoration," or "conversion." It is as if we saw a freshly bound up wound, or the mark of some arrested disease, or a wall newly raised out of its ruins.

And yet, as we look around us and within, we feel that this psalm would have been unreal if it had been all green pastures, still waters, comfort, repose, and peace; we feel that we know more about a barren and dry land where no water is, of a broken hedge, and poisonous herbs. There are thorns still clinging to our quivering flesh, stains still fresh upon our baptismal robe. Does the good Shepherd know anything of the waste land beyond the wilful gap? Are those pathless tracks trodden by His feet? Does the wild and howling wilderness know His gentle voice?

Yes, if He has appealed to my love as the good Shepherd of the green pastures, even more does He claim my adoration, my reverence, my heart, as the Shepherd of the lost and straying sheep. And yet, here there is no mention of sin, not a word of complaint for the ingratitude, the despised home, the forsaken path, the broken hedge, the wilful rushing away into the night. The psalmist says quite naturally, "He restoreth my soul." He has done it so often, so often fetched me back, so often seen me coming, and run to meet me, so often brought forth the robe, the ring, the shoes, the fatted calf, so often bowed down His shoulders, that we expect it again and again. "He restoreth my soul." Take care! Each time it is harder to turn, each time the weight is heavier; there are such things as "the losses of the saved."

I.

There is no disguising the fact, hide it as we will, of our frequent falling away. It seems almost incredible that it should be so. At our last confession we saw our sin in all its hideousness—that besetting sin, the sin which had galled us so long—and gently and mercifully it was untwined, all the trailing briar which had wound itself down from the cruel tree, and had torn us, wounded, and hindered us. We saw it snapped and disentangled, and broken at our feet—cut off. And we started away so light-hearted and free. Is it possible that already we can have gone, and flaunted ourselves once more, unheeding, beneath its tearing spikes; that again, of our own free action, we are torn, bleeding and maimed? When perhaps at the last moment of solemn resolution we saw everything so clearly before us, the right, the true, the high path, and visions of heaven, and heavenly things swept across us; but now it is the old story—

"*Video meliora proboque,
Deteriora sequor,*"

even if there be not an unconscious shrinking from the high standard which we have put before ourselves.

We are, after all, only face to face with an old difficulty, a well-known truth—the intense difficulty of holiness—διὸ καὶ ἔργον ἐστι σπουδαῖον εἶναι.[1]

Be it the weakness of our human nature, ever prone to evil; be it the corrupted atmosphere in which we live, the swampy marsh of the world, from which rises up, in stealthy, deadly fumes, the vapour of bad public opinion, which we call the world, where the mosses are brightest, and the flowers the fairest, and the sunbeams dance the merriest; be it Satan, above all, with his terrible power of trickery and deceit;—whatever it may be, try as hard as we may, we have to reckon with a constant deflection from a high ideal; if it be only the falling off in little things, where the pendulum of our life, as the machinery is allowed to run down, does not get so far in its transit backwards and forwards as it once did, does not touch meditation or midday prayer which it once used to reach, and then, getting slacker and slower, by degrees stops altogether; the will has

---

[1] Aristotle, "Ethics," ii. 9. 2.

ceased to act upon it. And perhaps we are happy if it be only this; it is more than likely, if we have dropped so far, that we have to bewail times when our will has snapped under pressure, when with our own hands we have broken down the hedge of rule, and turned our eyes away from the green pastures, and shut our ears to all restraining voices, and plunged into sin, only to lie bruised and shattered by that which we so rightly describe as a fall.

"He restoreth my soul." People have sometimes said about confession, "Is it not a rather dangerous thing? Do you not get into a habit of sinning and confessing, of confessing and sinning, with melancholy and unheeding regularity? Is not too frequent confession a spiritual snare?"

Let us only suppose that we are going to live in a very unhealthy country, such as the swamps and morasses of Central Africa; will the friend who gives us the medicine-chest say when he gives it, "Arrange with yourself now how often you will take the medicine, and don't take it too often"? You know, as a matter of fact, that you will have to take it as often as the fever comes upon you and leaves behind its deadly weakness. So with confession; it is perhaps right that we should make our confession without contemplating that we shall ever need to make another. And yet, as the days go on, and we find, to our consternation, weakness still asserting itself, again and again the old habit reappearing, with some fresh symptom, some hitherto undeveloped malignity, we are constrained to say, "Alas! I need it again. In vain do I plunge on, with faltering steps; the climate is too much for me. I have fallen below my own standard. My sins have taken such hold upon me that I am not able to look up. 'O send down Thine hand from above;' 'Set me up upon the rock that is higher than I.'" THEN "He restoreth my soul."

And all along the course of our life, His efforts to restore us, to help us to persevere, are spread out. Think only of the many new beginnings which He offers to us. The oft-recurring strength of our Communion, the storehouse of Sundays, the manifold means of grace which surround our path, are well known to us. But think, also, of such things as the disposition of day and night, the necessity of sleep, and the like: these are all merciful new beginnings which offer us occasions for fresh efforts after amendment. "We can have no thought what we should lose if we could dispense with sleep, and prolong day into day, by the loss of new beginnings.

> 'New every morning is the love
> Our wakening and uprising prove;
> Through sleep and darkness safely brought,
> Restored to life, and power, and thought.
>
> 'New blessings, each succeeding day,
> Hover around us while we pray;
> New perils past, new sins forgiven,
> New thoughts of God, new hopes of heaven.'

What a world of life and strength there is in that fresh self-oblation every morning! What a mercy to have had yesterday past, with its weariness and its failures and its burdens; to have had its venial sins washed out by the Lord's Prayer, and to begin anew with self-devotion to Jesus! What a life there is, if we be not in reach of, or do not venture upon actual Communion, in that first spiritual Communion, when God the Holy Ghost came into our souls, like the air which we breathe—yes, the very and eternal God!"[1]

[1] "Addresses to the Companions of the Love of Jesus," Dr. Pusey, pp. 4, 5.

It is so with the Church's seasons, with the great round of fast and festival, each with a fresh aspect of Divine grace, each with a fresh hope of a better life. As if each and all, linked in long procession, proclaimed the strain, "O come hither, and hearken, all ye that fear God: and I will tell you what He hath done for *thy* soul."[1] So, "He restoreth my soul."

II.

And being restored, once more the paths of righteousness lay open before us—the paths which come from righteousness, which end in righteousness, and are righteousness. Certainly we ought to strive for a more harmonious life of goodness. Our lives are too often sharply divided up, as you might divide a concert, into sacred and secular. And you especially, to whom the sacred ministry is opening up with all its splendid opportunities, —ought you not to try and consecrate all your life to God; to widen the path of righteousness, so that whether you eat or drink, or

[1] Ps. lxvi. 14.

whatsoever you do, all may be done to the glory of God?

Most certainly we should all strive to live by rule. It is impossible to over-estimate the importance of rule. Rule makes us like Jesus Christ, to Whom every action apparently had its hour, and Whose whole life was a fulfilment of minute prophecy. Rule forces our life into the shape of the cross. The cross must be upon our meals, in the self-restraint of a rule, which rigorously keeps them to the purpose for which they were intended, the support of the body. Our devotions also must be marked with the cross, in the vigorous effort to keep in check the waywardness of the will, the extravagance of the imagination, and the rebellion of the body. All life must be marked with the cross, as they had learned to do it who lived much in God's presence. "When thou art on the point of stepping over the threshold of thy door, utter this word first: 'I renounce thee, Satan, and thy pomp and thy service, and I enrol myself under Thee, O Christ.' Do thou never go out without this word; this shall be to thee a staff, a shield, an impregnable tower. And with this word form thou also the cross upon thy forehead; for so not only no man meeting thee, but not even the devil himself, can hurt thee."[1]

Rule, once more, helps us to utilize life. It is the scaffolding from which all the materials which daily life brings us can be placed upon the wall. The great stones are brought in by our rule of devotion and work, the sand is brought in by our rule of recreation, the rubbish is carted in by our rule of self-restraint. Righteousness, we may well believe, thus meaning the rule of a well-regulated life, earnest in purpose, fervent in prayer; whose shining path is guarded by the fortresses of devotion which lie on each side of it, while ejaculatory prayer, like the watchful sentry, patrols the space between.

The paths of righteousness, the very highest paths, are open to us; our very sins may be stepping-stones to higher things, and produce, if not humility, at least watchfulness. There, out of that fetid jungle, we have been able to bring the sweet flower of gentleness, which has sprung up, where bright vegetation has decayed around it; while sympathy and

[1] S. Chrysostom, quoted by Mr. Keble, "Eucharistical Adoration," p. 29.

tenderness for others shine forth in every word we speak, in every action that we do, as those who cannot afford to be severe in reference to the hundred pence, who are conscious of a forgiven debt of ten thousand talents.

"*Tu es Petrus.*" There is the design of character sketched in the boldest strokes on the uneven site, and crash after crash follows any attempt to build. "Get thee behind Me, Satan: thou art an offence to Me."[1] "When he was come into the house, Jesus prevented him;"[2] he had spoken without asking his Master. "O thou of little faith, wherefore didst thou doubt?"[3] "Then Simon Peter having a sword drew it, and smote the high priest's servant, and cut off his right ear."[4] "Then began he to curse and to swear."[5] "Simon, son of Jonas, lovest thou Me?"[6] Surely we may see, surface after surface, thrown up by a strong character, bits of sand and rubbish, unfit for foundation, broken down ruthlessly, remorselessly, until the bare rock is reached. Presumption is but an ex-

---

[1] S. Matt. xvi. 23.
[2] S. Matt. xvii. 25.
[3] S. Matt. xiv. 31.
[4] S. John xviii. 10.
[5] S. Matt. xxvi. 71.
[6] S. John xxi. 15.

crescence on courage, impulse on love, temerity on readiness.

So with us; He will bring out the character, if only we do not hinder Him, until it becomes established in righteousness.

III.

And this will He do "for His Name's sake." "The revealed Name, which gathers up and expresses for man just so much as he can apprehend of the Divine nature." That Name of which it is said, "*Deus quatenus ab hominibus invocatur celebratur.*"

His Name is Jesus. As great conquerors are named after their victories, so He is named from His. "He shall save;" "able to save;" "mighty to save." Through Jesus is the way to escape. This, perhaps, is Satan's chief terror which he holds over us— the impossibility of escape. "When so many mighty men have fallen"—it is his constant menace—"shalt thou be delivered?" while at the same time the whole Church system which our blessed Lord has left us, while it witnesses to His love, proclaims and cries out to our weakness, "How shall we escape, if we neglect?"[1]

His Name is *Emmanuel*, "God with us:" with us, in every stage of our life; with us, when we broke away; with us, when we came back; with us, as we were gaining strength, when the shorn locks of wilfulness began to grow again under returning faithfulness. "This God is our God for ever and ever: He shall be our Guide unto death."[1]

His Name is the Christ, the Prophet Who warns me, the Priest Who atones for me, the King Who rules me.

So He restoreth my soul; so He leads me in the paths of righteousness; so He pledges to me the assurance of His Holy Name."

[1] Heb. ii. 3.   [1] Ps. xlviii. 13.

IV.

"Yea, though I walk through the valley of the shadow of death, I will fear no evil: for Thou art with me; Thy rod and Thy staff they comfort me."—Ps. xxiii. 4.

THE wandering sheep has been brought back, without a word, without a murmur or reproach, by the restoring, the converting power of Christ. He has pledged Himself to do it, in virtue of that Holy Name—Jesus, Emmanuel, Christ, the Lord. The sheep is once more walking in the paths of righteousness, restored, pardoned, comforted. But still, beside and beyond the vast howling wilderness on each side of us, apart from the broken hedge and piercing thorn, there lies right in front of us a great shadow. The green pastures are darkened by it; the everlasting hills rise beyond it. There is no path visible at the base of it, but blackness and gloom are shed forth around it, with the bright sunshine still beyond. And the good

Shepherd leads on towards it. What can He do here?

It is death.

Is it wrong, this fear of death? Is it want of faith? Is it a childlike fear of the darkness? Will my faith stand it at the last? When I enter that shadow, will the darkness come in, even unto my soul?

Now, this verse is full of comfort; its very terms are reassuring. Death has become, certainly to us Christians, that which the psalmist imagined here—only a shadow. It is dark, cold, gloomy, terrible, but only a shadow. So said Archbishop Laud on the scaffold, "Lord, I am coming as fast as I can. I know I must pass through the shadow of death before I can come to see Thee. But it is but *umbra mortis*, a shadow of death, a little darkness upon nature; but Thou, Lord, by Thy goodness, hast broken the jaws and the power of death."[1]

Yes, our blessed Lord passed through the valley of death; we through the valley of the shadow of death. He tasted death[2] that we might never taste of it. He died that we might fall asleep. Yet, indeed, it is a great

[1] Quoted by Dr. Neale, Comment. *in loc.*   [2] Heb. ii. 9.

shadow; we see it as we watch, come waving out into the sunlight; and it lies with its thick folds for one moment on some sunny spot, and lo! as the shadow sinks back again something is gone. See it coursing along the mountain-side — now approaching, now receding! It is a shade full of separation, full of withered hopes and shattered joys.[1]

[1] Cf. the following beautiful passage in "Songs and Legends of Modern Greece," by Lady Verney, quoted in the *Contemporary Review*, December, 1875:—

"Why are the mountains black? Why are they charged with tears?
Is it that the wind does battle with them? Is it that the rain beats on them?
It is not the wind that fights with them, nor the rain that beats upon them;
It is only that Charon is passing with the dead.
He sends the young ones on in front, the old men behind,
And the tender little children are ranged in files upon his saddle.
The old men implore him, the young ones beseech him:
'My Charon, halt by the village, pause by some cool spring,
That the old men may drink the water, and the young may play with the disk,
And the tiny little children may gather the flow'rets.'
'I will not pause at the village, nor by the cool spring;
For the mothers coming there for the water would know their children again,
And the husbands and the wives would recognize each other, and it
Would not be possible to separate them.'"

And we are drawing nearer to it, and its cold chills and numbs us. "They feared as they entered into the cloud."[1] But a Form comes to meet us out of the gloom. "Fear not," He says; "for I am with thee." Here, too, it holds good, "The Lord is my Shepherd; I shall not want." He comes to meet my fears, to calm my apprehensions, to soothe my dread.

I.

"Thou art with me." I have eagerly seized on this; for out of all the terrors which gather themselves into the name of death, one has stood forth as a champion-fear to terrify and daunt me. It is the loneliness of death. "I die alone."

> "Jesu, have mercy!
> 'Tis this new feeling, never felt before,
> (Be with me, Lord, in my extremity!)
> That I am going, that I am no more.
> 'Tis this strange innermost abandonment,
> (Lover of souls! great God! I look to Thee,)
> This emptying out of each constituent
> And natural force, by which I come to be.

---

[1] S. Luke ix. 34.

> Pray for me, O my friends : a visitant
> Is knocking his dire summons at my door,
> The like of whom, to scare me and to daunt,
> Has never, never come to me before."[1]

Now, loneliness is a thing which we must learn to face, in our work, in the separations of life, and in times of quiet. Certainly, whether we like it or not, we must be alone in death, as far as this world is concerned. And men preach to us detachment. "Sit loosely to the world," they say, that the wrench may be less when it comes. But the good Shepherd says rather, learn attachment. It is His promise : "Fear not ; I will be with thee." It is our confidence : "I will fear no evil : for Thou art with me." Nay, more ; it is our joy : "Who shall separate us from the love of Christ ?"[2] And is not this the true answer to our fears—How can I go to meet that shadow ? How will my faith stand its cold embrace ? How shall I ever believe in the bright promise of a land beyond, when here all is dark ? Let us ask rather—How am I going to meet the duty just before me ? Is He with me now ? Have I learned to find Him in the quiet hours of the day ? Have I

---

[1] "Dream of Gerontius," § 1.   [2] Rom. viii. 35.

found His presence in desolating sorrow? Have I felt His hand in darkness and doubt? Have I found Him near me in prayer and Eucharist? If so, I need not look forward. He is leading me on, step by step, and day by day. He is habituating me, little by little, to the withdrawal of the light, and to utter trust in Him. "Sufficient unto the day is the evil thereof." There is grace given me for the new day's work; there is grace given me under this desolating sorrow. There is grace given me to live well; when I need it, there will be grace given me to die well. "For Thou art with me." Now is the time to make firm that companionship. To be still, and know that He is God. To find the guiding Hand in all its strength and security, amid the death and life of each day's hopes and fears. And then, when we enter the shadow, still it will be "with God onwards."

II.

"Thy rod and Thy staff they comfort me." What is this? The rod to correct, the staff to support; the two together forming the Holy Cross. So that the cross of punishment becomes the cross of our support. And we remember in the old history, when the little child was dead, how the prophet sent on his servant to lay his staff on the face of the child.[1] So here, in the solitude and desolation of the soul, when we look up and see that compassionate Form bending over us—"with us" in all the depth of His sympathy, "with us" to catch the fragments of broken prayers which escape our lips, "with us" to cheer and soothe—we hear Him say, "Is any sick among you? let him call for the elders of the Church; and let them pray over him."[2] Let them leave the altar at which they have been interceding. Let them leave the ninety and nine just persons who have been joining with them in the service of the Church, and let them come to the one sorely stricken sheep, whose wants, whose woes, and suffering demand the tender love of God. Let them come with their sympathy to one who deeply needs it, and with the authority of the Church, sent by Christ; and let them lay the rod and the staff of Christ upon the face of the dying man—the rod of His healing power, the staff

[1] 2 Kings iv. 18, etc.   [2] S. James v. 14.

of His supporting grace. So they come, sent by Christ, as His ambassadors, charged with His message, and bearing His comfort; to gather up the links of a shattered life, and bind them to the living Church, with its strong faith to support its mighty utterance, to carry up the enfeebled thoughts, in the sympathetic grace and power of its consecrated prayers. But more than this, the dying man lies crushed and broken. The priest can comfort him and help him by fervent prayer; but also this hour, the hour of approaching death, is the time of the soul's greatest agony of remorse. The curtain of mist between us and the other world is lifted here and there; there shoot out rays, and darting shafts of dazzling and awful brightness. And then it dawns upon the poor soul more than ever it did before, "I am a sinner about to meet my God;" "I am unclean; I go to stand before my Judge." There are tangled edges, and dark scars, and hideous seams, and blurred and blotted lines, running all round the frequent absolutions of my life. As a leper before the gathering light, I cry out, "Unclean, unclean!" As a suppliant before my Saviour, my heart cries out, "Lord, if Thou wilt, Thou canst make me clean." It is a supreme and awful moment, we may well believe. In the old tale which charmed our childhood, Crœsus, in his degradation, in his strange reverse, called out thrice from his funeral pyre the name of the old philosopher who had visited him in his prosperity; and being asked what he meant, he replied that Solon had told him many things which had all come true, and, among others, this saying, " Count no man happy while he lives." We can see the impression made by this utterance on the ancient world; it comes up again and again in poetry, and in the writings of the moralists; while more than one meaning has been found for it. And surely, beside the obvious truth, that life is subject to reverses, and that the end may stultify the beginning, there is also this truth contained in it, which we do well to consider; that at the hour of death we see life as we never saw it before; that we look back and see all things at last in their due perspective—pleasure and pain, hopes and failures, sins and blessings, mirrored before us by a miracle of memory, and all assuming their right and due proportion; then we can say, what we never could say before, whether life was happy or not.

And, alas! the happiest life leaves much to the mercy of God, much which needs forgiveness.

> "When the tempter me pursueth
> With the sins of all my youth,
> And half damns me with untruth,
> Sweet Spirit, comfort me.
>
> "When the taper lights burn blue,
> And the comforters are few,
> And that number more than true,
> Sweet Spirit, comfort me.
>
> "When God knows I'm tost about
> Either with despair or doubt,
> Yet before the glass be out,
> Sweet Spirit, comfort me." [1]

Here, again, the rod and staff of Christ is there in the presence of His Church. The priest offers to the dying man the last pardon through the precious blood of Jesus. Then, when the trembling lips can scarce articulate the confession; then, when the brain is crowded and agitated with thronging, jostling turmoil of memories; then, "when the heart is sad within with the thought of all its sin;" then the priest of God is bidden once more to

[1] Herrick, "Litany."

say those words of power and great comfort, "Our Lord Jesus Christ, Who hath left power to His Church to absolve all sinners who truly repent and believe in Him, of His great mercy forgive thee thine offences: and by His authority committed to me, I absolve thee from all thy sins, In the Name of the Father, and of the Son, and of the Holy Ghost. Amen." Many ties are being severed, at that moment, which bind the man to earth. Some are of silver, some of gold; these snap off, not without a pang. But what can it be but a sense of intense relief and unspeakable joy to be freed from the chain of defilement, the chain of bondage, the chain of infirmity, with which Satan has bound us through the weary years of a struggling life?

But is there nothing else? Has the priest no more in his hands? Cheered by prayer, loosened from sin's chains, the spirit still has death to face. Must we break off abruptly? Must we garble Holy Scripture? Or may we go on to say, "anointing him with oil in the Name of the Lord"?[1] In other days, and still in other branches of the Church, there is the anointing with holy oil, bestowed

[1] S. James v. 14.

upon the sick man, after the practice of the Apostles, and according to the precept of S. James. Who has deprived us of this privilege? Is the Church of England maimed of her rights, and her children of their consolation, in this their need? Shall we say, Holy Unction is "the lost Pleiad of the Anglican firmament"?[1] The facts, briefly, are these. Our Lord's Apostles anointed the sick with oil, to heal their bodies and to heal their souls. The Holy Spirit by S. James orders the elders of the Church to carry out this rule—to anoint the sick, to the healing of the body, if it be God's will, and to the healing of the wounded soul, to soothe the scars, as yet barely closed over. But, on leaving the actual pages of Holy Scripture, it is difficult to trace this rite as a distinct ministration of the Church until the fifth century. After this, it appears in the Middle Ages, surrounded with abuses; and it passed with other things under the hands of the Reformers; when, in the first Prayer-book of Edward VI., an office for the anointing of the sick was inserted, but was removed in a

---

[1] See for this expression, and on what follows, Forbes on Article XXV.

subsequent revision, and, alas! never afterwards restored. But still, even if this rite remains in abeyance, we need not think that we have parted altogether with the comfort of it, if the actual symbol of oil is gone. The outward sign is gone, it is true; but the healing ministry of the Church is there, and we may partake of the benefits of the ordinance in a manner analogous to a spiritual communion. The sick man seeks in faith for Christ through His Church; strength, blessing, guidance, grace, and healing if He will, are given. Still there is given to him the oil of grace, the oil which is to kindle the lamp to guide him to his heavenly Bridegroom. Still the soothing oil of healing is applied with the wine of the absolution, in the comfort spoken by the Church. Still the athlete is anointed with the last anointing before his great struggle in the arena, round which are gathered, tier upon tier, the great cloud of witnesses; albeit the oil be merely in the spiritual grace, not sealed or conferred by an outward sign. Still the good Shepherd confers the crowning blessing of life. He anoints the head with oil at Baptism, at Confirmation, at Ordination, and now at the hour of death.

And so the cup is full. He Who began the good work in the soul is performing it still, and will perform it until the great day. No; if we have lost any assurance of comfort, any outward means, let us hope and believe and know that it is made up to us, that we still receive the full grace of Christ in the last rites of the Church.[1]

But the rod and the staff of the cross have a further and a higher function still. There is the most comfortable food of the Body and Blood of Christ, the *Viaticum* now to be given. The darkness deepens, and He makes as though He would go further; and the sick man constrains Him, saying, "Abide with *me:* for it is toward evening, and the day is far spent."[2] And He enters in to tarry with him. In vain now are the assaults of Satan. He can only strike us through Christ Him-

---

[1] I have said nothing here as to the revival of unction. Dr. Pusey says in his "Eirenicon," p. 222, "Nor do I know of any ground, except the custom of the Church, why it should not be used in England." So, again, Bishop Forbes on Article XXV.: "There is nothing to hinder the revival of the Apostolic and Scriptural custom of anointing the sick whensoever any devout person may desire it. It is, indeed, difficult to say on what principle it could be refused."

[2] S. Luke xxiv. 29.

self. "Thou hast been a Strength to the poor, a Strength to the needy in his distress, a Refuge from the storm, a Shadow from the heat, when the blast of the terrible ones is as a storm against the wall."[1] The great Roman, in his magnificent self-confidence, cheered the frightened pilot in the storm, saying, "Fear not; you carry Cæsar." There is One with us, Whom we carry with us, Who can say as no one else can, as wave after wave of sorrow and anguish bursts over our heads, "It is I; be not afraid."[2]

III.

And it is for us His ministers to remember that the good Shepherd may call upon us thus to carry His staff, that we may lay it upon the face of the sick man, at any moment. Surely this is one reason why many things, not harmful in themselves, may yet be unclerical. It strikes a discordant note if the staff is brought to us, shall we say, in the hunting-field, or when we are dressed up in some strange costume for the purpose of a game. "There is somebody dying!" "There is no time to

[1] Isa. xxv. 4. [2] S. Matt. xiv. 27.

lose!" "Come at once!" "Come and pray!" "Come and give him the last consolations of the dying!" Was the failure on the part of Elisha's messenger connected in any way with the character of Gehazi? People, rightly or wrongly, shrink from the ministrations of their clergy on personal grounds sometimes.

It is a point we should think well over, for it seems doubtful whether a priest can ever be really "off duty." For life, once more, is not divisible into sacred and secular; it is all sacred. And the very recreation of the priest is the recreation of one who may be summoned at any moment to stand very near to that cold, waving shadow, to concentrate all his powers on saving a soul alive. Much cause is there for him to look to it that men do not for his fault abhor the offering of the Lord.

V.

"Thou preparest a table before me in the presence of mine enemies: Thou anointest my head with oil; my cup runneth over."—Ps. xxiii. 5.

THERE would seem to be three black lines of sorrow, which run across this vision of peace.

Already we have looked into that dark region of falls and weakness which opened up to us, with the mention of restoration and conversion. From this He brings us back.

Death in His hands, as we gazed with Him into its black cavernous gloom, became a shadow.

But there still remains a third trouble. Even in the green pastures, so fresh and bright, even where the waters of comfort go rippling on their way, even where the paths of righteousness lie evenly between the hedges, there linger "mine enemies," or, as we more familiarly call them, "those that trouble us;" and we can think of so many.

I.

First, there are temptations, commonly so called, which can be a trouble, even when they have ceased to be a dread, just at the moment when we are enjoying the beauty of the scene.

> "It is a beauteous evening, calm and free;
> The holy time is quiet as a nun
> Breathless with adoration; the broad sun
> Is sinking down in its tranquillity;
> The gentleness of heaven is on the sea."

Just when all is peace and glory, there comes the ribald murmur of an evil thought, the haunting disquiet of some evil imagination. In a moment the vast unprotected surface of the mind is ruffled and clouded as with a storm-gust, and pitted with stinging suggestions of falling evil. Most certainly "those that trouble us" take the shape of evil thoughts.

Or doubts, again, rise up at the most solemn moments, at some turning-point in our path. "This steep road cannot be right. The higher path of duty is a mistake. The view of uninterrupted splendour which I have promised myself will never come! The path leads nowhither; it is but a sheep-track, beaten by the tramp of uninquiring generations. I am the slave of an imposture, the victim of a cunningly devised fable." Doubts are certainly among those that trouble us.

And then there is the constant weakness, the weariness of the road, the faintness which makes us stumble, the distaste for prayer, the distractions which perplex us. These, again, are things which trouble us; and anxiously we turn to the good Shepherd. Can He help us? Is He any protection against these lesser trials of life, these flies and gnats of temptation, whose very littleness and persistency make up a serious burden?

But, cry as I may, not one disappears; not even the thorn in the flesh, which seems so utterly disabling and so flagrantly cruel. No, my enemies stand all round me; they buzz about my ears; they settle; they sting. "Why go I thus heavily while the enemy oppresseth me?"

He does not concern Himself with them; He is busying Himself about me. The way lies through obstacles more and even greater than these. It is not His care to remove temptation, but to strengthen the tempted. He never promised to remove trouble; but

He has promised to make anxiety out of the question. He never promised to remove pain; but He has promised to elevate it into a bearing, supporting cross. "He prepares a table before me in the presence of mine enemies," as they stand like a lion greedy of his prey, casting their eyes down to the ground. "They kept me in, I say, on every side;" "The ungodly walk on every side;" "Lord, how are they increased that trouble me!"

II.

And what is this table, so strange, so unexpected, prepared in the presence of enemies thirsting for my life?

Pre-eminently, it speaks to a Christian of the Blessed Sacrament of the Lord's Body and Blood. In a wider meaning, it is our Holy Religion. It represents all those different ways and means of grace in which God strengthens us against temptation. He knows how strong temptation is, and must be, if we are to be fitted to enter heaven; and knowing whereof we are made, remembering that we are but dust, He gives us something against it, a table prepared in the presence of our enemies.

If, then, we are to push our way through these obstacles, He would seem to say that above all things it is necessary that religion should preoccupy the soul; it is the empty soul that is so mercilessly tormented. A man that has no principle, no settled religious beliefs, no settled religious obligations, who depends on his surroundings and companions, it is he who is so mercilessly tormented. It is all-important that we should be definite—definite in faith, definite in life, definite in practice; hence the great importance of laying in a good foundation. It sounds very well, and it trades upon the great names of liberality, moderation, charity, and toleration, to be indefinite; but we must remember that there are times when a man's salvation depends on the exact knowledge of the truth. He is lying by the roadside in a fit, or bleeding to death. A sympathetic crowd stand round him; some are giving him remedies which are quite wrong; all mean well; but a doctor comes by who knows exactly the right thing to do, and he saves life. Perhaps, while we are devising all sorts of plans and schemes for ourselves, it is some simple Church food that we want. A man, for instance, may go on making resolutions, and taking precautions against sin, which confession would set right; or struggling to regain his strength, when it is the food of the Holy Eucharist which alone can nourish him. Let us never be afraid of the Church's plan; it is the plain truth laid down for us; it is God's table prepared against the very troubles of life, and in their presence. The poor man by the wayside was healed of his wounds; but he found at the inn of the Church the table prepared, that he should go forth stronger and better to meet the difficulties of the way.

And no less in "the table" do we trace a provision of strength. Over and over again Holy Scripture appeals to us with warning voice, "Be strong." God knows the strain which we have to undergo, the unhealthy atmosphere, the miasmatic plain, the poisonous swamps and jungles through which the path winds, and therefore He prepares a table of strength. In these hurrying days, there is a tendency to multiply results of any sort, so that they be results, rather than to strengthen that which produces results; to work away without stopping to sharpen, clean, or replenish the instrument; to judge time spent in devotion as so much time wrested from the important and pressing business of life.

But do not let us work before we have received strength to produce the work. Saul must wait for Samuel; he will do better when he comes.[1] "Thou canst not follow Me now; but thou shalt follow Me afterwards."[2] We must wait. People grudge us our Daily Service; they grumble at our frequent Celebrations. It becomes a subtle temptation, as with a man who is short of money to economize his charities, so when we are short of time to economize in our devotions. But it is a bad policy. What strength we might have, if we made use of this table of religion! We should go from morning to midday, from midday to evening, from evening to night, from night to morning, strengthened by a force from within. We should find ourselves a source of strength to all around us. Let us remember nothing will ever make up for want of holiness, and

[1] 1 Sam. xiii.   [2] S. John xiii. 36.

holiness is only kept alive by the sustenance of the King's table.

And yet, again, the table is a feast of good things. There is the intense interest of religious life and religious work. Worldly men cannot understand it, simply because they have not thrown themselves into it. It would seem to be a fact that our enjoyment of everything is in direct proportion to the interest which we bestow upon it, and to the extent in which we devote ourselves to it. Even the very games and recreations of life are insipid when we cannot play them, or neglect to enter into them. "The joy of the Lord is your strength."[1] See how joyful, how bright, God is all around us in His marvellous works. See how those who have caught something of His Spirit—the enthusiasts, as we call them—feel and know the same joy. Is it the mountaineer, who is toiling all day amidst fatigue, danger, and hardship, exulting in it? Is it the naturalist grubbing in a ditch, rejoicing as treasure after treasure opens itself before his educated eye? Look at the scholar, blinding himself, as he pores over his books; or the discoverer, in

[1] Neh. viii. 10.

his wild εὕρηκα; or the doctor in some interesting case, which is taxing all his energies, and exhausting his nervous powers. All these have enthusiasm. And has religion none, think you? Ah, you have found it out already! Are there not glorious views to be seen in meditation? Are there not flowers to be culled out of the dark deep ditch of penitence, which only grow there? Is there no enthusiasm in work, the joy over one sinner that repenteth; in the wrestling with sin and with the ravages of Satan?

Do not let us despise enthusiasms; they carry us on. They are a table of delight, prepared in the presence of our enemies. Enthusiasm, at least, helps us not to feel. "He that dies in an earnest pursuit is like one that is wounded in hot blood, who for the time scarce feels the hurt; and therefore a mind fixed and bent upon something that is good, doth avert the dolour of death!"

III.

And as the angels came and ministered to Christ after His temptation, so the anointed head and the replenished cup speak of the joy and gladness which wait on those who overcome. There is the oil of joy and grace, poured over our heads, which makes us prophets, priests, and kings of God to all those with whom we are brought into contact. Prophets, who speak out of an atmosphere of life and holiness ; priests, who minister of the consolation wherewith they themselves are comforted of God ; kings, natural chiefs among men, in the evenness, gentleness, and peace of a well-ordered life.

And at the end there comes the full cup. Everything contributes to the store of wealth, all things work together for good, because we love God. Life in all its changes, health, prosperity, affliction, all add to the great store of blessing, and God's mercy fills the cup of happiness to overflowing. God grant that our lives may overflow with His mercies, fertilizing as we go. As trees and verdure in the desert proclaim from afar the little spot where water is, so around our Churches may there gather the beauty of devotion and the signs of progress ; may the refreshing water, as it drops out of the full cup, lap over, and in its path arise the schools for the young, the refuge for the fallen, and the Christian homes, all dwelling within sound of its soft murmur, all so many trees planted by the water-side, which may bring forth their fruit in due season.

> " Be noble, and the nobleness that lies
> In other men, sleeping, but never dead,
> Will rise in majesty to meet thine own ;
> Then wilt thou see it gleam in many eyes,
> Then will pure light around thy path be shed,
> And thou wilt never more be sad and lone."

VI.

"Surely goodness and mercy shall follow me all the days of my life: and I will dwell in the house of the Lord for ever."—Ps. xxiii. 6.

THIS verse coming at the end of the psalm is full of blessing. It is like the great "Lo, I am with you alway, even unto the end of the world. Amen."[1] After the falls of the third verse, after the fears of the fourth, after the temptations of the fifth, still it is "goodness and mercy" that he has to think of. "My song shall be alway of the lovingkindness of the Lord: with my mouth will I ever be shewing Thy truth from one generation to another."[2]

And there seems to be an air of security in this verse; of final perseverance and of final safety; of difficulties overcome, of troubles outlived, of fears dispersed; of a constant, abiding Presence; of a sure and fixed dwell-

[1] S. Matt. xxviii. 20.   [2] Ps. lxxxix. 1

ing-place; of a rest that remaineth; of safety from the fear of the evil one. "Surely goodness and mercy shall follow me all the days of my life: and I will dwell in the house of the Lord for ever."

I.

At once these words, "goodness and mercy," attract our attention. It was "goodness and mercy" that led us first out of the fold, with an aim and object in life. There was "goodness and mercy" in that shelter from the noontide heat. But now it is "goodness and mercy" all the days of my life. And we think of grace which is not only preventing and accompanying, but also subsequent. We owe a great deal to the grace that comes after, the grace that follows us; the grace that not only gives us the wish to do what is right, not only the grace that starts us and helps us in what is right, but also the grace which helps us to finish.

Here is that striking characteristic of the love of God Almighty which comes out in all His dealings with us, namely, its completeness. "Having loved His own which were in the world, He loved them unto the end."[1] Creative love, which placed man in the world, did not exhaust the goodness of God towards us: Redemptive love met him when he fell. And as if Redemptive love itself were not sufficient, Sanctifying love came in to fill up where Redemptive love seemed to lack. So it is with each single soul. God completes His work.

And, indeed, we all need this following grace, this persistent love of God. Think of that which is so graphically described in the psalms as "the wickedness of my heels" which "compasseth me round about."[2] Think how much misery and trouble come to us from past sins, attacking the heels of life. How many would faint and fail, if God's grace did not follow them! So, when S. Peter went out into the night, God's grace followed him, and at last brought him back through his tears and sorrow. When S. Thomas forsook the first Christian assembly, God's lovingkindness followed him, and helped his lagging faith. When many a soul is struggling with good, God comes between him and evil with His following grace.

[1] S. John xiii. 1.   [2] Ps. xlix. 5.

"The glory of the Lord shall be thy rereward."[1] Here, indeed, is a mercy that follows us all the days of our life.

Nor is this all. Look at what we are pleased to call our best actions: how imperfect they are, how poor, how wretched! How can they be accepted but by the merits and mediation of Jesus Christ? Or, look how ready we are to give up! How soon we get tired! How soon we get wearied of the wilderness! How few would reach the Promised Land were it not that we are able to drink of that Rock which follows us, and that Rock is Christ!

"Lord, we pray Thee that Thy grace may always prevent and follow us."[1] We toil in rowing until Jesus comes; we cannot cast out the devil until He comes to us from the mountain; Lazarus lies dead in the grave until Christ's voice brings life into the tomb; the Scriptures are dumb until He opens our understanding, that we may know their depth. It is an experience of power, of confidence, and hope, to feel that One is following us in the tenderness of an everlasting love.

[1] Isa. lviii. 8.
[2] Collect for Seventeenth Sunday after Trinity.

II.

"And I will dwell in the house of the Lord for ever." It is your hope and desire, and, please God, it will be your privilege, to dwell much in the house of the Lord. You will have frequently to go there, to plead the great Sacrifice. Day by day you will have to go into the Holy Place to offer the incense. It will be yours to kindle the lamp of a never-ceasing devotion, to place the Eucharistic Shewbread before the Lord. You will have to learn to stand before that dread Presence, to lift the veil, to come forth to the people to bless, to wield the mighty power of the keys, to linger much and long in His courts. Then, when the very presence of your infirmity casts a shadow of defilement; then, when the full rush of prayers and supplications flow by in a full tide—

> "We two will stand beside that shrine,
>   Occult, withheld, untrod,
> Whose lamps are stirred continually
>   With prayer sent up to God;
> And see our old prayers granted, melt
>   Each like a little cloud."

I hope that we, if any, shall make the house of God our home; that we shall see that its door is always open, and that it is well cared for; that its services are frequent, and that we often go in and out of it; that we try and make it the home for the town or village; and a place where all will be welcome. A disused church is always repelling. The parish church should be the golden milestone from which we measure our parochial journeys; its clock should be the ruler of our time; its chimes be our call to hourly prayer, as it tells out the history of the day; its tower, or roof, be a constraining presence, as we walk up and down within view of it; its altar the centre of our universe. The psalmist would rather be a doorkeeper in the house of the Lord than dwell in the tents of ungodliness. "Blessed are they that dwell in Thy house," he bursts out: "they will be alway praising Thee."[1] Here it is your privilege to dwell. "Rise, and measure the temple of God," says the angel, "and the altar, and them that worship therein."[2] Measure, that is to extend it, take in more temple. And this is an especial call to the priest. Make your life all temple, all part of the τεμένος, the sacred enclosure. Enlarge it

[1] Ps. lxxxiv. 4.   [2] Rev. xi. 1.

towards the east, where we look for our Saviour's coming. Let it be a life of patient witness for God. Enlarge it towards the west, where the sun of our life is gently dipping towards the grave, in a life of preparedness. Enlarge it towards the north, on the frontier of Satan. Enlarge it towards the sunny south; take in many a piece of ground which is now covered by worldly occupations, business, or pleasure. The priest's temple, the priest's life, the priest's house of God, it is the sacred enclosure of Israel, to which the actual house of God is the holy of holies. "I will dwell in the house of the Lord for ever." This should be our aim, to attain to the realization of the life hid with Christ in God; and to this God is separating us off, that our sojourn with Him may be eternal. For this He separated us at Baptism from our old corrupt nature; for this He measured us off at Confirmation, cutting us away from our surroundings, that He might bring us to Himself, by the indwelling power of His Holy Spirit. So He separates us off at each Holy Communion, by self-examination, repentance, and resolution; so He separates us off at many a special time of good desire;

times when we have visions of the plan, and can see the house of the Lord, with its turrets and walls, and soaring pinnacles, in its beauty and completeness. And now again at Ordination, the angel with the measuring-line in his hand will come and take still more for the house of God; our time, our reading, our recreation, our thoughts, our aims. Surely now, if there is any evil habit; short of this, if there is any idle habit; short of this, if there is any unconsecrated habit;—let us resolve to take in ground for God. You remember in old days, when the conquering enemy thundered at the gates of Rome, flushed with victory and red with slaughter, how the ground on which he stood was bought and sold by the citizens of that very city which he came to destroy. Before they had routed him, before they had rolled back that armed and arrogant conqueror, the very ground on which he stood changed owners in a commercial transaction. So, in view of your Ordination, see to it that you buy Satan's camp, the world's camp, the flesh's camp. Let us plant our stakes and measuring-lines there, and so take in ground for God—more room for the house of the Lord.

III.

"The house of the Lord for ever." The days are coming when God Himself will measure the temple, His house; to see who are His, and who shall dwell in His tabernacle. It is the permanence of heaven that is one of its greatest joys in prospect. It is an abiding place, a mansion. There is no restoring there, no troubling there; no dark misty shade of death to chill the sunlight of the road. And the joy of heaven is surely the presence of God, the presence of the saints, the freedom from temptation, sin, and sorrow, for ever.

Heaven may begin here. The priest, if any, may come to closer and closer visions of God. It is he to whose awful lot it falls to say these words, "This is My Body," "This is My Blood." It is he who has to stand beside the penitent, and convey to him the pardon through the precious Blood of a present Lord. He has to go with his Master to many a dying man, to many a sick and afflicted soul, to many a one wounded in life's battle.

The priest, if any, is sustained by the sense

of the communion of saints; he has the words of saints on his lips; he ministers in buildings consecrated, many of them, by the piety of ages. He finds records of past holiness and past work in his parish. He is ever looking to the examples of the saints of old to sustain him.

He knows, if any, where temptation can be overthrown, and how sorrow can be met.

And so heaven begins here, and his life of heaven here on earth melts into the life of heaven hereafter. His prayers, his work, his ministry, his recreation, his time here and his time hereafter, become one great house of the Lord, in which, by the goodness and favour of the good Shepherd, he abides for ever.

PRINTED BY WILLIAM CLOWES AND SONS, LIMITED,
LONDON AND BECCLES.

A Catalogue of Works

in

THEOLOGICAL LITERATURE

PUBLISHED BY

Messrs. LONGMANS, GREEN, & CO.

39 Paternoster Row, London, E.C.

Abbey and Overton.—THE ENGLISH CHURCH IN THE EIGHTEENTH CENTURY. By Charles J. Abbey, M.A., Rector of Checkendon, Reading, and John H. Overton, M.A., Rector of Epworth, Doncaster, Rural Dean of Isle of Axholme. *Cr. 8vo. 7s. 6d.*

Adams.—SACRED ALLEGORIES. The Shadow of the Cross—The Distant Hills—The Old Man's Home—The King's Messengers. By the Rev. William Adams, M.A. *Crown 8vo. 5s.*

The Four Allegories may be had separately, with Illustrations. 16mo. 1s. each. Also the Miniature Edition. Four Vols. 32mo. 1s. each; in a box, 5s.

Aids to the Inner Life.

Edited by the Rev. W. H. Hutchings, M.A., Rector of Kirkby Misperton, Yorkshire. *Five Vols. 32mo, cloth limp, 6d. each; or cloth extra, 1s. each. Sold separately.*
Also an Edition *with red borders, 2s. each.*

OF THE IMITATION OF CHRIST. By Thomas à Kempis. In Four Books.

THE CHRISTIAN YEAR: Thoughts in Verse for the Sundays and Holy Days throughout the Year.

THE DEVOUT LIFE. By St. Francis de Sales.

THE HIDDEN LIFE OF THE SOUL. From the French of Jean Nicolas Grou.

THE SPIRITUAL COMBAT. Together with the Supplement and the Path of Paradise. By Laurence Scupoli.

Andrewes.—A MANUAL FOR THE SICK; with other Devotions. By Lancelot Andrewes, D.D., sometime Bishop of Winchester. With Preface by H. P. Liddon, D.D. *24mo. 2s. 6d.*

Augustine.—THE CONFESSIONS OF ST. AUGUSTINE. In Ten Books. Translated and Edited by the Rev. W. H. HUTCHINGS, M.A. *Small 8vo.* 5s. *Cheap Edition.* 16mo. 2s. 6d.

Bathe.—Works by the Rev. ANTHONY BATHE, M.A.
A LENT WITH JESUS. A Plain Guide for Churchmen. Containing Readings for Lent and Easter Week, and on the Holy Eucharist. 32mo, 1s.; *or in paper cover*, 6d.
WHAT I SHOULD BELIEVE. A Simple Manual of Self-Instruction for Church People. *Crown 8vo.* 3s. 6d.

Bickersteth.—Works by EDWARD HENRY BICKERSTETH, D.D., Bishop of Exeter.
THE LORD'S TABLE; or, Meditations on the Holy Communion Office in the Book of Common Prayer. 16mo. 1s.; *or cloth extra*, 2s.
YESTERDAY, TO-DAY, AND FOR EVER: a Poem in Twelve Books. *One Shilling Edition,* 18mo. *With red borders,* 16mo, 2s. 6d.
The Crown 8vo Edition (5s.) *may still be had.*

Blunt.—Works by the Rev. JOHN HENRY BLUNT, D.D.
DICTIONARY OF DOCTRINAL AND HISTORICAL THEOLOGY. By various Writers. Edited by the Rev. JOHN HENRY BLUNT, D.D. *Imperial 8vo.* 21s.
DICTIONARY OF SECTS, HERESIES, ECCLESIASTICAL PARTIES AND SCHOOLS OF RELIGIOUS THOUGHT. By various Writers. Edited by the Rev. JOHN HENRY BLUNT, D.D. *Imperial 8vo.* 21s.
THE BOOK OF CHURCH LAW. Being an Exposition of the Legal Rights and Duties of the Parochial Clergy and the Laity of the Church of England. Revised by Sir WALTER G. F. PHILLIMORE, Bart., D.C.L. *Crown 8vo.* 7s. 6d.
A COMPANION TO THE BIBLE: Being a Plain Commentary on Scripture History, to the end of the Apostolic Age. *Two vols. small 8vo. Sold separately.*
THE OLD TESTAMENT. 3s. 6d.   THE NEW TESTAMENT. 3s. 6d.
HOUSEHOLD THEOLOGY: a Handbook of Religious Information respecting the Holy Bible, the Prayer Book, the Church, the Ministry, Divine Worship, the Creeds, etc. etc. *Paper cover*, 16mo. 1s. Also the Larger Edition, 3s. 6d.

Body.—Works by the Rev. GEORGE BODY, D.D., Canon of Durham.
THE SCHOOL OF CALVARY; or, Laws of Christian Life revealed from the Cross. A Course of Lectures delivered in substance at All Saints', Margaret Street. *Crown 8vo.* 3s. 6d.
THE LIFE OF JUSTIFICATION: a Series of Lectures delivered in substance at All Saints', Margaret Street. 16mo. 2s. 6d.
THE LIFE OF TEMPTATION: a Course of Lectures delivered in substance at St. Peter's, Eaton Square; also at All Saints', Margaret Street. 16mo. 2s. 6d.

Boultbee.—A COMMENTARY ON THE THIRTY-NINE ARTICLES OF THE CHURCH OF ENGLAND. By the Rev. T. P. BOULTBEE, formerly Principal of the London College of Divinity, St. John's Hall, Highbury. *Crown 8vo.* 6s.

Bright.—Works by WILLIAM BRIGHT, D.D., Canon of Christ Church.
LESSONS FROM THE LIVES OF THREE GREAT FATHERS: St. Athanasius, St. Chrysostom, and St. Augustine. *Crown 8vo.* 6s.
THE INCARNATION AS A MOTIVE POWER. *Crown 8vo.* 6s.
IONA AND OTHER VERSES. *Small 8vo.* 4s. 6d.
HYMNS AND OTHER VERSES. *Small 8vo.* 5s.
FAITH AND LIFE: Readings for the greater Holy Days, and the Sundays from Advent to Trinity. Compiled from Ancient Writers. *Small 8vo.* 5s.

Bright and Medd.—LIBER PRECUM PUBLICARUM ECCLESIÆ ANGLICANÆ. A GULIELMO BRIGHT, S.T.P., et PETRO GOLDSMITH MEDD, A.M., Latine redditus. [In hac Editione continentur Versiones Latinæ—1. Libri Precum Publicarum Ecclesiæ Anglicanæ; 2. Liturgiæ Primæ Reformatæ; 3. Liturgiæ Scoticanæ; 4. Liturgiæ Americanæ.] *Small 8vo.* 7s. 6d.

Browne.—AN EXPOSITION OF THE THIRTY-NINE ARTICLES, Historical and Doctrinal. By E. H. BROWNE, D.D., formerly Bishop of Winchester. *8vo.* 16s.

Campion and Beamont.—THE PRAYER BOOK INTERLEAVED. With Historical Illustrations and Explanatory Notes arranged parallel to the Text. By W. M. CAMPION, D.D., and W. J. BEAMONT, M.A. *Small 8vo.* 7s. 6d.

Carter.—Works edited by the Rev. T. T. CARTER, M.A., Hon. Canon of Christ Church, Oxford.
THE TREASURY OF DEVOTION: a Manual of Prayer for General and Daily Use. Compiled by a Priest. 18mo. 2s. 6d.; *cloth limp*, 2s.; *or bound with the Book of Common Prayer*, 3s. 6d. *Large-Type Edition. Crown 8vo.* 5s.
THE WAY OF LIFE: A Book of Prayers and Instruction for the Young at School, with a Preparation for Confirmation. Compiled by a Priest. 18mo. 1s. 6d.
THE PATH OF HOLINESS: a First Book of Prayers, with the Service of the Holy Communion, for the Young. Compiled by a Priest. With Illustrations. 16mo. 1s. 6d.; *cloth limp*, 1s.
THE GUIDE TO HEAVEN: a Book of Prayers for every Want. (For the Working Classes.) Compiled by a Priest. 18mo. 1s. 6d.; *cloth limp*, 1s. *Large-Type Edition. Crown 8vo.* 1s. 6d.; *cloth limp*, 1s.

[*continued.*

Carter.—Works edited by the Rev. T. T. CARTER, M.A., Hon. Canon of Christ Church, Oxford—*continued.*
   SELF-RENUNCIATION. From the French. 16mo. 2s. 6d. Also the Larger Edition. Small 8vo. 3s. 6d.
   THE STAR OF CHILDHOOD; a First Book of Prayers and Instruction for Children. Compiled by a Priest. With Illustrations. 16mo. 2s. 6d.

Carter.—MAXIMS AND GLEANINGS FROM THE WRITINGS OF T. T. CARTER, M.A. Selected and arranged for Daily Use. Crown 16mo. 2s.

Compton.—THE ARMOURY OF PRAYER. A Book of Devotion. Compiled by the Rev. BERDMORE COMPTON, M.A. 18mo. 3s. 6d.

Conybeare and Howson.—THE LIFE AND EPISTLES OF ST. PAUL. By the Rev. W. J. CONYBEARE, M.A., and the Very Rev. J. S. HOWSON, D.D. With numerous Maps and Illustrations.
   LIBRARY EDITION. *Two Vols.* 8vo. 21s.
   STUDENT'S EDITION. *One Vol.* Crown 8vo. 6s.

Crake.—HISTORY OF THE CHURCH UNDER THE ROMAN EMPIRE, A.D. 30–476. By the Rev. A. D. CRAKE, B.A. Crown 8vo. 7s. 6d.

Creighton.—HISTORY OF THE PAPACY DURING THE REFORMATION. By MANDELL CREIGHTON, D.D., LL.D., Bishop of Peterborough. 8vo. *Vols. I. and II.*, 1378-1464, 32s. *Vols. III. and IV.*, 1464-1518, 24s.

Devotional Series, 16mo, Red Borders. *Each* 2s. 6d.
   BICKERSTETH'S YESTERDAY, TO-DAY, AND FOR EVER.
   CHILCOT'S EVIL THOUGHTS.
   CHRISTIAN YEAR.
   DEVOTIONAL BIRTHDAY BOOK.
   HERBERT'S POEMS AND PROVERBS.
   KEMPIS' (À) OF THE IMITATION OF CHRIST.
   ST. FRANCIS DE SALES' THE DEVOUT LIFE.
   WILSON'S THE LORD'S SUPPER. *Large type.*
   *TAYLOR'S (JEREMY) HOLY LIVING.
   *———   ———   HOLY DYING.
        These two in one Volume. 5s.

Devotional Series, 18mo, without Red Borders. *Each* 1s.
   BICKERSTETH'S YESTERDAY, TO-DAY, AND FOR EVER.
   CHRISTIAN YEAR.
   KEMPIS' (À) OF THE IMITATION OF CHRIST.
   WILSON'S THE LORD'S SUPPER. *Large type.*
   *TAYLOR'S (JEREMY) HOLY LIVING.
   *———   ———   HOLY DYING.
        These two in one Volume. 2s. 6d.

Edersheim.—Works by ALFRED EDERSHEIM, M.A., D.D., Ph.D., sometime Grinfield Lecturer on the Septuagint, Oxford.

    THE LIFE AND TIMES OF JESUS THE MESSIAH. *Two Vols.* 8vo. 24s.

    JESUS THE MESSIAH : being an Abridged Edition of 'The Life and Times of Jesus the Messiah.' *Crown 8vo. 7s. 6d.*

    PROPHECY AND HISTORY IN RELATION TO THE MESSIAH : The Warburton Lectures, 1880-1884. 8vo. 12s.

    TOHU-VA-VOHU ('Without Form and Void') : being a collection of Fragmentary Thoughts and Criticism. *Crown 8vo. 6s.*

Ellicott.—Works by C. J. ELLICOTT, D.D., Bishop of Gloucester and Bristol.

    A CRITICAL AND GRAMMATICAL COMMENTARY ON ST. PAUL'S EPISTLES. Greek Text, with a Critical and Grammatical Commentary, and a Revised English Translation. 8vo.

    1 CORINTHIANS. 16s.
    GALATIANS. 8s. 6d.
    EPHESIANS. 8s. 6d.
    PASTORAL EPISTLES. 10s. 6d.
    PHILIPPIANS, COLOSSIANS, AND PHILEMON. 10s. 6d.
    THESSALONIANS. 7s. 6d.

    HISTORICAL LECTURES ON THE LIFE OF OUR LORD JESUS CHRIST. 8vo. 12s.

Epochs of Church History. Edited by MANDELL CREIGHTON, D.D., LL.D., Bishop of Peterborough. *Fcap. 8vo. 2s. 6d. each.*

THE ENGLISH CHURCH IN OTHER LANDS. By the Rev. H. W. TUCKER, M.A.

THE HISTORY OF THE REFORMATION IN ENGLAND. By the Rev. GEO. G. PERRY, M.A.

THE CHURCH OF THE EARLY FATHERS. By the Rev. ALFRED PLUMMER, D.D.

THE EVANGELICAL REVIVAL IN THE EIGHTEENTH CENTURY. By the Rev. J. H. OVERTON, M.A.

THE UNIVERSITY OF OXFORD. By the Hon. G. C. BRODRICK, D.C.L.

THE UNIVERSITY OF CAMBRIDGE. By J. BASS MULLINGER M.A.

THE ENGLISH CHURCH IN THE MIDDLE AGES. By the Rev. W. HUNT, M.A.

THE CHURCH AND THE EASTERN EMPIRE. By the Rev. H. F. TOZER, M.A.

THE CHURCH AND THE ROMAN EMPIRE. By the Rev. A. CARR.

THE CHURCH AND THE PURITANS, 1570-1660. By HENRY OFFLEY WAKEMAN, M.A.

HILDEBRAND AND HIS TIMES By the Rev. W. R. W. STEPHENS, M.A

THE POPES AND THE HOHENSTAUFEN. By UGO BALZANI.

THE COUNTER-REFORMATION. By ADOLPHUS WILLIAM WARD, Litt. D

WYCLIFFE AND MOVEMENTS FOR REFORM. By REGINALD L. POOLE, M.A.

THE ARIAN CONTROVERSY. By H. M. GWATKIN, M.A.

Fosbery.—Works edited by the Rev. THOMAS VINCENT FOSBERY, M.A., sometime Vicar of St. Giles's, Reading.

VOICES OF COMFORT. *Cheap Edition. Small 8vo. 3s. 6d.*
The Larger Edition (7s. 6d.) may still be had.

HYMNS AND POEMS FOR THE SICK AND SUFFERING. In connection with the Service for the Visitation of the Sick. Selected from Various Authors. *Small 8vo. 3s. 6d.*

Garland.—THE PRACTICAL TEACHING OF THE APOCALYPSE. By the Rev. G. V. GARLAND, M.A. *8vo. 16s.*

Gore.—Works by the Rev. CHARLES GORE, M.A., Principal of the Pusey House; Fellow of Trinity College, Oxford.

THE MINISTRY OF THE CHRISTIAN CHURCH. *8vo. 10s. 6d.*
ROMAN CATHOLIC CLAIMS. *Crown 8vo. 3s. 6d.*

Goulburn.—Works by EDWARD MEYRICK GOULBURN, D.D., D.C.L., sometime Dean of Norwich.

THOUGHTS ON PERSONAL RELIGION. *Small 8vo, 6s. 6d.*; *Cheap Edition, 3s. 6d.*; *Presentation Edition, 2 vols. small 8vo, 10s. 6d.*

THE PURSUIT OF HOLINESS: a Sequel to 'Thoughts on Personal Religion.' *Small 8vo. 5s. Cheap Edition, 3s. 6d.*

THE CHILD SAMUEL: a Practical and Devotional Commentary on the Birth and Childhood of the Prophet Samuel, as recorded in 1 Sam. i., ii. 1-27, iii. *Small 8vo. 2s. 6d.*

THE GOSPEL OF THE CHILDHOOD: a Practical and Devotional Commentary on the Single Incident of our Blessed Lord's Childhood (St. Luke ii. 41 to the end). *Crown 8vo. 2s. 6d.*

THE COLLECTS OF THE DAY: an Exposition, Critical and Devotional, of the Collects appointed at the Communion. With Preliminary Essays on their Structure, Sources, etc. *2 vols. Crown 8vo. 8s. each.*

THOUGHTS UPON THE LITURGICAL GOSPELS for the Sundays, one for each day in the year. With an Introduction on their Origin, History, the Modifications made in them by the Reformers and by the Revisers of the Prayer Book. *2 vols. Crown 8vo. 16s.*

MEDITATIONS UPON THE LITURGICAL GOSPELS for the Minor Festivals of Christ, the two first Week-days of the Easter and Whitsun Festivals, and the Red-letter Saints' Days. *Crown 8vo. 8s. 6d.*

FAMILY PRAYERS compiled from various sources (chiefly from Bishop Hamilton's Manual), and arranged on the Liturgical Principle. *Crown 8vo. 3s. 6d. Cheap Edition. 16mo. 1s.*

Haddan.—APOSTOLICAL SUCCESSION IN THE CHURCH OF ENGLAND. By the Rev. ARTHUR W. HADDAN, B.D., late Rector of Barton-on-the-Heath. *8vo. 12s.*

Hatch.—THE ORGANIZATION OF THE EARLY CHRISTIAN CHURCHES. Being the Bampton Lectures for 1880. By Edwin Hatch, M.A., D.D. *8vo. 5s.*

Hernaman.—LYRA CONSOLATIONIS. From the Poets of the Seventeenth, Eighteenth, and Nineteenth Centuries. Selected and arranged by Claudia Frances Hernaman. *Small 8vo. 6s.*

Holland.—Works by the Rev. Henry Scott Holland, M.A., Canon and Precentor of St. Paul's.

CREED AND CHARACTER : Sermons. *Crown 8vo. 7s. 6d.*

ON BEHALF OF BELIEF. Sermons preached in St. Paul's Cathedral. *Crown 8vo. 6s.*

CHRIST OR ECCLESIASTES. Sermons preached in St. Paul's Cathedral. *Crown 8vo. 3s. 6d.*

GOOD FRIDAY. Being Addresses on the Seven Last Words, delivered at St. Paul's Cathedral on Good Friday. *Small 8vo. 2s.*

LOGIC AND LIFE, with other Sermons. *Crown 8vo. 7s. 6d.*

Hopkins.—CHRIST THE CONSOLER. A Book of Comfort for the Sick. By Ellice Hopkins. *Small 8vo. 2s. 6d.*

James.—COMMENT UPON THE COLLECTS appointed to be used in the Church of England on Sundays and Holy Days throughout the Year. By John James, D.D., sometime Canon of Peterborough. *Small 8vo. 3s. 6d.*

Jameson.—Works by Mrs. Jameson.

SACRED AND LEGENDARY ART, containing Legends of the Angels and Archangels, the Evangelists, the Apostles, the Doctors of the Church, St. Mary Magdalene, the Patron Saints, the Martyrs, the Early Bishops, the Hermits, and the Warrior-Saints of Christendom, as represented in the Fine Arts. With 19 etchings on Copper and Steel, and 187 Woodcuts. *Two Vols. Cloth, gilt top, 20s. net.*

LEGENDS OF THE MONASTIC ORDERS, as represented in the Fine Arts, comprising the Benedictines and Augustines, and Orders derived from their Rules, the Mendicant Orders, the Jesuits, and the Order of the Visitation of S. Mary. With 11 etchings by the Author, and 88 Woodcuts. *One Vol. Cloth, gilt top, 10s. net.*

LEGENDS OF THE MADONNA, OR BLESSED VIRGIN MARY. Devotional with and without the Infant Jesus, Historical from the Annunciation to the Assumption, as represented in Sacred and Legendary Christian Art. With 27 Etchings and 165 Woodcuts. *One Vol. Cloth, gilt top, 10s. net.*

THE HISTORY OF OUR LORD, as exemplified in Works of Art, with that of His Types, St. John the Baptist, and other Persons of the Old and New Testaments. Commenced by the late Mrs. Jameson; continued and completed by Lady Eastlake. With 31 etchings and 281 Woodcuts. *Two Vols. 8vo. 20s. net.*

Jennings.—ECCLESIA ANGLICANA. A History of the Church of Christ in England from the Earliest to the Present Times. By the Rev. ARTHUR CHARLES JENNINGS, M.A. *Crown 8vo.* 7s. 6d.

Jukes.—Works by ANDREW JUKES.
 THE NEW MAN AND THE ETERNAL LIFE. Notes on the Reiterated Amens of the Son of God. *Crown 8vo.* 6s.
 THE NAMES OF GOD IN HOLY SCRIPTURE: a Revelation of His Nature and Relationships. *Crown 8vo.* 4s. 6d.
 THE TYPES OF GENESIS. *Crown 8vo.* 7s. 6d.
 THE SECOND DEATH AND THE RESTITUTION OF ALL THINGS. *Crown 8vo.* 3s. 6d.
 THE MYSTERY OF THE KINGDOM. *Crown 8vo.* 2s. 6d.

Keble.—MAXIMS AND GLEANINGS FROM THE WRITINGS OF JOHN KEBLE, M.A. Selected and Arranged for Daily Use. By C. M. S. *Crown 16mo.* 2s.
 SELECTIONS FROM THE WRITINGS OF JOHN KEBLE, M.A. *Crown 8vo.* 3s. 6d.

Kennaway.—CONSOLATIO; OR, COMFORT FOR THE AFFLICTED. Edited by the late Rev. C. E. KENNAWAY. *16mo.* 2s. 6d.

Knox Little.—Works by W. J. KNOX LITTLE, M.A., Canon Residentiary of Worcester, and Vicar of Hoar Cross.
 THE CHRISTIAN HOME. *Crown 8vo.*
 THE HOPES AND DECISIONS OF THE PASSION OF OUR MOST HOLY REDEEMER. *Crown 8vo.* 3s. 6d.
 THE THREE HOURS' AGONY OF OUR BLESSED REDEEMER. Being Addresses in the form of Meditations delivered in St. Alban's Church, Manchester, on Good Friday, 1877. *Small 8vo.* 2s.; *or in Paper Cover,* 1s.
 CHARACTERISTICS AND MOTIVES OF THE CHRISTIAN LIFE. Ten Sermons preached in Manchester Cathedral, in Lent and Advent 1877. *Crown 8vo.* 3s. 6d.
 SERMONS PREACHED FOR THE MOST PART IN MANCHESTER. *Crown 8vo.* 7s. 6d.
 THE MYSTERY OF THE PASSION OF OUR MOST HOLY REDEEMER. *Crown 8vo.* 3s. 6d.
 THE WITNESS OF THE PASSION OF OUR MOST HOLY REDEEMER. *Crown 8vo.* 3s. 6d.
 THE LIGHT OF LIFE. Sermons preached on Various Occasions. *Crown 8vo.* 7s. 6d.
 SUNLIGHT AND SHADOW IN THE CHRISTIAN LIFE. Sermons preached for the most part in America. *Crown 8vo.* 7s. 6d.

Lear.—Works by, and Edited by, H. L. SIDNEY LEAR.

    CHRISTIAN BIOGRAPHIES. *Crown 8vo. 3s. 6d. each.*

        MADAME LOUISE DE FRANCE, Daughter of Louis XV., known also as the Mother Térèse de St. Augustin.

    FOR DAYS AND YEARS. A Book containing a Text, Short Reading, and Hymn for Every Day in the Church's Year. 16mo. 2s. 6d. *Also a Cheap Edition*, 32mo. 1s.; *or cloth gilt*, 1s. 6d.

    FIVE MINUTES. Daily Readings of Poetry. 16mo. 3s. 6d. *Also a Cheap Edition.* 32mo. 1s.; *or cloth gilt*, 1s. 6d.

    WEARINESS. A Book for the Languid and Lonely. *Large Type.* Small 8vo. 5s.

    THE LIGHT OF THE CONSCIENCE. 16mo. 2s. 6d. *Also the Larger Edition.* Crown 8vo. 5s.

- A DOMINICAN ARTIST: a Sketch of the Life of the Rev. Père Besson, of the Order of St. Dominic.
- HENRI PERREYVE. By A. GRATRY.
- ST. FRANCIS DE SALES, Bishop and Prince of Geneva.
- THE REVIVAL OF PRIESTLY LIFE IN THE SEVENTEENTH CENTURY IN FRANCE.
- A CHRISTIAN PAINTER OF THE NINETEENTH CENTURY.
- BOSSUET AND HIS CONTEMPORARIES.
- FÉNELON, ARCHBISHOP OF CAMBRAI.
- HENRI DOMINIQUE LACORDAIRE.

    DEVOTIONAL WORKS. Edited by H. L. SIDNEY LEAR. *New and Uniform Editions. Nine Vols.* 16mo. 2s. 6d. *each.*

- FÉNELON'S SPIRITUAL LETTERS TO MEN.
- FÉNELON'S SPIRITUAL LETTERS TO WOMEN.
- A SELECTION FROM THE SPIRITUAL LETTERS OF ST. FRANCIS DE SALES.
- THE SPIRIT OF ST. FRANCIS DE SALES.
- THE HIDDEN LIFE OF THE SOUL.
- THE LIGHT OF THE CONSCIENCE.
- SELF-RENUNCIATION. From the French.
- ST. FRANCIS DE SALES' OF THE LOVE OF GOD.
- SELECTIONS FROM PASCAL'S THOUGHTS.

Library of Spiritual Works for English Catholics. *Original Edition. With Red Borders. Small 8vo. 5s. each. New and Cheaper Editions.* 16mo. 2s. 6d. *each.*

    OF THE IMITATION OF CHRIST.

    THE SPIRITUAL COMBAT. By LAURENCE SCUPOLI.

    THE DEVOUT LIFE. By ST. FRANCIS DE SALES.

    OF THE LOVE OF GOD. By ST. FRANCIS DE SALES.

    THE CONFESSIONS OF ST. AUGUSTINE. *In Ten Books.*

    THE CHRISTIAN YEAR. 5s. *Edition only.*

Liddon.—Works by HENRY PARRY LIDDON, D.D., D.C.L., LL.D., late Canon Residentiary and Chancellor of St. Paul's.

THE DIVINITY OF OUR LORD AND SAVIOUR JESUS CHRIST. Being the Bampton Lectures for 1866. *Crown 8vo. 5s.*

ADVENT IN ST. PAUL'S. Sermons bearing chiefly on the Two Comings of our Lord. *Two Vols. Crown 8vo. 5s. each. Cheap edition in one Volume. Crown 8vo. 5s.*

CHRISTMASTIDE IN ST. PAUL'S. Sermons bearing chiefly on the Birth of our Lord and the End of the Year. *Crown 8vo. 5s.*

PASSIONTIDE SERMONS. *Crown 8vo. 5s.*

EASTER IN ST. PAUL'S. Sermons bearing chiefly on the Resurrection of our Lord. *Two Vols. Crown 8vo. 5s. each. Cheap Edition in one Volume. Crown 8vo. 5s.*

SERMONS PREACHED BEFORE THE UNIVERSITY OF OXFORD. *Two Vols. Crown 8vo. 5s. each. Cheap Edition in one Volume. Crown 8vo. 5s.*

THE MAGNIFICAT. Sermons in St. Paul's. *Crown 8vo. 2s. 6d.*

SOME ELEMENTS OF RELIGION. Lent Lectures. *Small 8vo. 2s. 6d.*; or in Paper Cover, 1s. 6d.
The Crown 8vo Edition (5s.) may still be had.

SELECTIONS FROM THE WRITINGS OF H. P. LIDDON, D.D. *Crown 8vo. 3s. 6d.*

MAXIMS AND GLEANINGS FROM THE WRITINGS OF H. P. LIDDON, D.D. Selected and arranged by C. M. S. *Crown 16mo. 2s.*

Littlehales.—Works Edited by HENRY LTTLEHALES.

A FOURTEENTH CENTURY PRAYER BOOK: being Pages in Facsimile from a Layman's Prayer Book in English about 1400 A.D. *4to. 3s. 6d.*

THE PRYMER OR PRAYER-BOOK OF THE LAY PEOPLE IN THE MIDDLE AGES. In English, dating about 1400 A.D. Part I. Text. *Royal 8vo. 5s.*

Luckock.—Works by HERBERT MORTIMER LUCKOCK, D.D., Canon of Ely.

AFTER DEATH. An Examination of the Testimony of Primitive Times respecting the State of the Faithful Dead, and their Relationship to the Living. *Crown 8vo. 6s.*

THE INTERMEDIATE STATE BETWEEN DEATH AND JUDGMENT. Being a Sequel to *After Death. Crown 8vo. 6s.*

FOOTPRINTS OF THE SON OF MAN, as traced by St. Mark. Being Eighty Portions for Private Study, Family Reading, and Instructions in Church. *Two Vols. Crown 8vo. 12s. Cheap Edition in one Vol. Crown 8vo. 5s.*

[*continued.*

Luckock.—Works by HERBERT MORTIMER LUCKOCK, D.D., Canon of Ely—*continued.*

    THE DIVINE LITURGY. Being the Order for Holy Communion, Historically, Doctrinally, and Devotionally set forth, in Fifty Portions. *Crown 8vo.* 6s.

    STUDIES IN THE HISTORY OF THE BOOK OF COMMON PRAYER. The Anglican Reform—The Puritan Innovations—The Elizabethan Reaction—The Caroline Settlement. With Appendices. *Crown 8vo.* 6s.

    THE BISHOPS IN THE TOWER. A Record of Stirring Events affecting the Church and Nonconformists from the Restoration to the Revolution. *Crown 8vo.* 6s.

LYRA APOSTOLICA. Poems by J. W. BOWDEN, R. H. FROUDE, J. KEBLE, J. H. NEWMAN, R. I. WILBERFORCE, and I. WILLIAMS; and New Preface by CARDINAL NEWMAN. 16mo. 2s. 6d.

LYRA GERMANICA. Hymns translated from the German by CATHERINE WINKWORTH. *Small 8vo.* 5s.

MacColl.—CHRISTIANITY IN RELATION TO SCIENCE AND MORALS. By the Rev. MALCOLM MACCOLL, M.A., Canon Residentiary of Ripon. *Crown 8vo.* 6s.

Mason.—Works by A. J. MASON, D.D., formerly Fellow of Trinity College, Cambridge.

    THE FAITH OF THE GOSPEL. A Manual of Christian Doctrine. *Crown 8vo.* 7s. 6d. *Large-Paper Edition for Marginal Notes.* 4to. 12s. 6d.

    THE RELATION OF CONFIRMATION TO BAPTISM. As taught by the Western Fathers. A Study in the History of Doctrine. *Crown 8vo.*

Mercier.—Works by Mrs. JEROME MERCIER.

    OUR MOTHER CHURCH: being Simple Talk on High Topics. *Small 8vo.* 3s. 6d.

    THE STORY OF SALVATION: or, Thoughts on the Historic Study of the Bible. *Small 8vo.* 3s. 6d.

Moberly.—Works by GEORGE MOBERLY, D.C.L., late Bishop of Salisbury.

    PLAIN SERMONS. Preached at Brighstone. *Crown 8vo.* 5s.

    THE SAYINGS OF THE GREAT FORTY DAYS, between the Resurrection and Ascension, regarded as the Outlines of the Kingdom of God. In Five Discourses. *Crown 8vo.* 5s.

    PAROCHIAL SERMONS. Mostly preached at Brighstone. *Crown 8vo.* 7s. 6d.

    SERMONS PREACHED AT WINCHESTER COLLEGE. *Two Vols. Small 8vo.* 6s. 6d. *each.*

Mozley.—Works by J. B. MOZLEY, D.D., late Canon of Christ Church, and Regius Professor of Divinity at Oxford.

   ESSAYS, HISTORICAL AND THEOLOGICAL. *Two Vols.* 8vo. 24s.

   EIGHT LECTURES ON MIRACLES. Being the Bampton Lectures for 1865. *Crown 8vo.* 7s. 6d.

   RULING IDEAS IN EARLY AGES AND THEIR RELATION TO OLD TESTAMENT FAITH. Lectures delivered to Graduates of the University of Oxford. 8vo. 10s. 6d.

   SERMONS PREACHED BEFORE THE UNIVERSITY OF OXFORD, and on Various Occasions. *Crown 8vo.* 7s. 6d.

   SERMONS, PAROCHIAL AND OCCASIONAL. *Crown 8vo.* 7s. 6d.

Mozley.—Works by the Rev. T. MOZLEY, M.A., Author of 'Reminiscences of Oriel College and the Oxford Movement.'

   THE WORD. *Crown 8vo.* 7s. 6d.

   LETTERS FROM ROME ON THE OCCASION OF THE ŒCUMENICAL COUNCIL 1869-1870. *Two Vols. Cr. 8vo.* 18s.

Newbolt.—Works by the Rev. W. C. E. NEWBOLT, Canon Residentiary of St. Paul's.

   THE FRUIT OF THE SPIRIT. Being Ten Addresses bearing on the Spiritual Life. *Crown 8vo.* 2s. 6d.

   THE MAN OF GOD. Being Six Addresses delivered during Lent 1886, at the Primary Ordination of the Right Rev. the Lord Alwyne Compton, Bishop of Ely. *Small 8vo.* 1s. 6d.

   COUNSELS OF FAITH AND PRACTICE. Being Sermons preached on Various Occasions. 8vo. 7s. 6d.

   THE VOICE OF THE PRAYER BOOK. Being Spiritual Addresses bearing on the Book of Common Prayer. *Crown 8vo.* 2s. 6d.

Newnham.—THE ALL-FATHER : Sermons preached in a Village Church. By the Rev. H. P. NEWNHAM. With Preface by EDNA LYALL. *Crown 8vo.* 4s. 6d.

Newman.—Works by JOHN HENRY NEWMAN, B.D. (Cardinal Newman), formerly Vicar of St. Mary's, Oxford.

   PAROCHIAL AND PLAIN SERMONS. *Eight Vols. Cabinet Edition. Crown 8vo.* 5s. *each. Popular Edition. Eight Vols. Crown 8vo.* 3s. 6d. *each.*

                                                               [continued.

Newman.—Works by JOHN HENRY NEWMAN, B.D. (Cardinal Newman), formerly Vicar of St. Mary's, Oxford—*continued.*

SELECTION, ADAPTED TO THE SEASONS OF THE ECCLESIASTICAL YEAR, from the 'Parochial and Plain Sermons.' *Crown 8vo.* 5s.

FIFTEEN SERMONS PREACHED BEFORE THE UNIVERSITY OF OXFORD, between A.D. 1826 and 1843. *Crown 8vo.* 5s.

SERMONS BEARING UPON SUBJECTS OF THE DAY. *Crown 8vo.* 5s.

LECTURES ON THE DOCTRINE OF JUSTIFICATION. *Crown 8vo.* 5s.

*** *For other Works by Cardinal Newman, see Messrs. Longmans & Co.'s Catalogue of Works in General Literature.*

THE LETTERS AND CORRESPONDENCE OF JOHN HENRY NEWMAN DURING HIS LIFE IN THE ENGLISH CHURCH. With a Brief Autobiographical Memoir. Arranged and Edited by ANNE MOZLEY. *Two Vols.* 8vo. 30s. *net.*

Osborne.—Works by EDWARD OSBORNE, Mission Priest of the Society of St. John the Evangelist, Cowley, Oxford.

THE CHILDREN'S SAVIOUR. Instructions to Children on the Life of our Lord and Saviour Jesus Christ. *Illustrated.* 16mo. 3s. 6d.

THE SAVIOUR-KING. Instructions to Children on Old Testament Types and Illustrations of the Life of Christ. *Illustrated.* 16mo. 3s. 6d.

THE CHILDREN'S FAITH. Instructions to Children on the Apostles' Creed. *With Illustrations.* 16mo. 3s. 6d.

Oxenden.—Works by the Right Rev. ASHTON OXENDEN, formerly Bishop of Montreal.

THE PATHWAY OF SAFETY; or, Counsel to the Awakened. *Fcap. 8vo, large type.* 2s. 6d. Cheap Edition. *Small type, limp.* 1s.

THE EARNEST COMMUNICANT. Common Edition. 32mo. 1s. New Red Rubric Edition. 32mo. 2s.

OUR CHURCH AND HER SERVICES. *Fcap.* 8vo. 2s. 6d.

FAMILY PRAYERS FOR FOUR WEEKS. First Series. *Fcap.* 8vo. 2s. 6d. Second Series. *Fcap.* 8vo. 2s. 6d.

    LARGE TYPE EDITION. Two Series in one Volume. *Crown* 8vo. 6s.

COTTAGE SERMONS; or, Plain Words to the Poor. *Fcap.* 8vo. 2s. 6d.

THOUGHTS FOR HOLY WEEK. 16mo. 1s. 6d.

DECISION. 18mo. 1s. 6d.

[continued.

Oxenden.—Works by the Right Rev. ASHTON OXENDEN, formerly Bishop of Montreal—*continued.*

THE HOME BEYOND; or, A Happy Old Age. *Fcap. 8vo. 1s. 6d.*

THE LABOURING MAN'S BOOK. *18mo, large type, cloth. 1s. 6d.*

PEACE AND ITS HINDRANCES. *Cr. 8vo. 1s. paper cover; 2s. cloth.*

CONFIRMATION. *18mo, cloth, 9d; sewed, 3d.; or 2s. 6d. per dozen.*

COUNSELS TO THOSE WHO HAVE BEEN CONFIRMED; or, Now is the Time to serve Christ. *18mo, cloth. 1s.*

THE LORD'S SUPPER SIMPLY EXPLAINED. *18mo, cloth. 1s. Cheap Edition. Paper. 6d.*

PRAYERS FOR PRIVATE USE. *32mo, cloth. 1s.*

WORDS OF PEACE; or, The Blessings of Sickness. *16mo, cloth. 1s.*

Paget.—Works by the Rev. FRANCIS PAGET, D.D., Canon of Christ Church, and Regius Professor of Pastoral Theology.

THE SPIRIT OF DISCIPLINE: Sermons. *Crown 8vo. 6s. 6d.*

FACULTIES AND DIFFICULTIES FOR BELIEF AND DISBELIEF. *Crown 8vo. 6s. 6d.*

THE HALLOWING OF WORK. Addresses given at Eton, January 16-18, 1888. *Small 8vo. 2s.*

PRACTICAL REFLECTIONS. By a CLERGYMAN. With Prefaces by H. P. LIDDON, D.D., D.C.L. *Crown 8vo.*

    Vol. I.—THE HOLY GOSPELS. *4s. 6d.*
    Vol. II.—ACTS TO REVELATION. *6s.*
    THE PSALMS. *5s.*

PRIEST (THE) TO THE ALTAR; Or, Aids to the Devout Celebration of Holy Communion, chiefly after the Ancient English Use of Sarum. *Royal 8vo. 12s.*

Pusey.—Works by the late Rev. E. B. PUSEY, D.D.

MAXIMS AND GLEANINGS FROM THE WRITINGS OF EDWARD BOUVERIE PUSEY, D.D. Selected and Arranged for Daily Use. By C. M. S. *Crown 16mo. 2s.*

PRIVATE PRAYERS. With Preface by H. P. LIDDON, D.D. *32mo. 2s. 6d.*

PRAYERS FOR A YOUNG SCHOOLBOY. Edited, with a Preface, by H. P. LIDDON, D.D. *24mo. 1s.*

SELECTIONS FROM THE WRITINGS OF EDWARD BOUVERIE PUSEY, D.D. *Crown 8vo. 3s. 6d.*

Richmond.—CHRISTIAN ECONOMICS. By the Rev. WILFRID RICHMOND, M.A., sometime Warden of Trinity College, Glenalmond. *Crown 8vo.* 6s.

Sanday.—THE ORACLES OF GOD: Nine Lectures on the Nature and Extent of Biblical Inspiration and the Special Significance of the Old Testament Scriptures at the Present Time. By W. SANDAY, M.A., D.D., LL.D. *Crown 8vo.* 4s.

Seebohm.—THE OXFORD REFORMERS—JOHN COLET, ERASMUS, AND THOMAS MORE: A History of their Fellow-Work. By FREDERICK SEEBOHM. *8vo.* 14s.

Stephen.—ESSAYS IN ECCLESIASTICAL BIOGRAPHY. By the Right Hon. Sir J. STEPHEN. *Crown 8vo.* 7s. 6d.

Swayne.—THE BLESSED DEAD IN PARADISE. Four All Saints' Day Sermons, preached in Salisbury Cathedral. By ROBERT G. SWAYNE, M.A. *Crown 8vo.* 3s. 6d.

Tweddell.—THE SOUL IN CONFLICT. A Practical Examination of some Difficulties and Duties of the Spiritual Life. By MARSHALL TWEDDELL, M.A., Vicar of St. Saviour, Paddington. *Crown 8vo.* 6s.

Twells.—COLLOQUIES ON PREACHING. By HENRY TWELLS, M.A., Honorary Canon of Peterborough *Crown 8vo.* 5s.

Wakeman.—THE HISTORY OF RELIGION IN ENGLAND. By HENRY OFFLEY WAKEMAN, M.A. *Small 8vo.* 1s. 6d.

Welldon. — THE FUTURE AND THE PAST. Sermons preached to Harrow Boys. (*First Series*, 1885 *and* 1886.) By the Rev. J. E. C. WELLDON, M.A., Head Master of Harrow School. *Crown 8vo.* 7s. 6d.

Williams.—Works by the Rev. ISAAC WILLIAMS, B.D., formerly Fellow of Trinity College, Oxford.

A DEVOTIONAL COMMENTARY ON THE GOSPEL NARRATIVE. *Eight Vols. Crown 8vo.* 5s. *each. Sold separately.*

THOUGHTS ON THE STUDY OF THE HOLY GOSPELS.
A HARMONY OF THE FOUR GOSPELS.
OUR LORD'S NATIVITY.
OUR LORD'S MINISTRY (Second Year).
OUR LORD'S MINISTRY (Third Year).
THE HOLY WEEK.
OUR LORD'S PASSION.
OUR LORD'S RESURRECTION.

[continued.

Williams.—Works by the Rev. ISAAC WILLIAMS, B.D., formerly Fellow of Trinity College, Oxford—*continued.*

FEMALE CHARACTERS OF HOLY SCRIPTURE. A Series of Sermons. *Crown 8vo.* 5*s.*

THE CHARACTERS OF THE OLD TESTAMENT. A Series of Sermons. *Crown 8vo.* 5*s.*

THE APOCALYPSE. With Notes and Reflections. *Crown 8vo.* 5*s.*

SERMONS ON THE EPISTLES AND GOSPELS FOR THE SUNDAYS AND HOLY DAYS THROUGHOUT THE YEAR. Two Vols. *Crown 8vo.* 5*s. each.*

PLAIN SERMONS ON THE CATECHISM. Two Vols. *Crown 8vo.* 5*s. each.*

SELECTIONS FROM THE WRITINGS OF ISAAC WILLIAMS, B.D. *Crown 8vo.* 3*s.* 6*d.*

Woodford.—Works by JAMES RUSSELL WOODFORD, D.D., sometime Lord Bishop of Ely.

THE GREAT COMMISSION. Twelve Addresses on the Ordinal. Edited with an Introduction on the Ordinations of his Episcopate, by HERBERT MORTIMER LUCKOCK, D.D. *Crown 8vo.* 5*s.*

SERMONS ON OLD AND NEW TESTAMENT SUBJECTS. Edited by HERBERT MORTIMER LUCKOCK, D.D. Two Vols. *Crown 8vo.* 5*s. each.*

Woodruff.—THE CHILDREN'S YEAR. Verses for the Sundays and Holy Days throughout the Year. By C. H. WOODRUFF B.C.L. With an Introduction by the LORD BISHOP OF SOUTHWELL. *Fcap. 8vo.* 3*s.* 6*d.*

Wordsworth.—

For List of Works by the late Christopher Wordsworth, D.D., Bishop of Lincoln, see Messrs. Longmans & Co.'s Catalogue of Theological Works, 32 pp. Sent post free on application.

Wordsworth.—Works by ELIZABETH WORDSWORTH, Principal of Lady Margaret Hall, Oxford.

ILLUSTRATIONS OF THE CREED. *Crown 8vo.* 5*s.*

CHRISTOPHER AND OTHER POEMS. *Crown 8vo.* 6*s.*

Younghusband.—Works by FRANCES YOUNGHUSBAND.

THE STORY OF OUR LORD, told in Simple Language for Children. With 25 Illustrations on Wood from Pictures by the Old Masters, and numerous Ornamental Borders, Initial Letters, etc., from Longmans' New Testament. *Crown 8vo.* 2*s.* 6*d.*

THE STORY OF GENESIS, told in Simple Language for Children. *Crown 8vo.* 2*s.* 6*d.*

Printed by T. and A. CONSTABLE, Printers to Her Majesty, at the Edinburgh University Press.

www.ingramcontent.com/pod-product-compliance
Lightning Source LLC
Chambersburg PA
CBHW020254170426
43202CB00008B/367